HOOKED ON TRIANGLES

19 QUILTS FOR FOUNDATION PIECING

KRISTIN BERGLJOT JOHANNESSEN
and TURID MARGARET UREN

Martingale®
& COMPANY

Dedication

To our hometown of Bergen, Norway, and all the eager quilters who live there. When we started out very small back in 1986, you came to be part of this new and exciting craft brought to us from the United States. Thank you for taking our classes, buying our fabric, and joining a sisterhood that has given us many hours of joyful togetherness and brought us new friends from near and far.

Photo by Gunnar Strøm

Credits

President ▲ *Nancy J. Martin*
CEO ▲ *Daniel J. Martin*
Publisher ▲ *Jane Hamada*
Editorial Director ▲ *Mary V. Green*
Managing Editor ▲ *Tina Cook*
Technical Editor ▲ *Laurie Baker*
Copy Editor ▲ *Ellen Balstad*
Design Director ▲ *Stan Green*
Illustrator ▲ *Laurel Strand*
Cover and Text Designer ▲ *Trina Stahl*
Photographer ▲ *Brent Kane*

That Patchwork Place® is an imprint of Martingale & Company®.

Mission Statement

Dedicated to providing quality products and service to inspire creativity.

Hooked on Triangles: 19 Quilts for Foundation Piecing
© 2004 by Kristin Bergljot Johannessen and Turid Margaret Uren

Martingale & Company
20205 144th Avenue NE
Woodinville, WA 98072-8478 USA
www.martingale-pub.com

Printed in China
09 08 07 06 05   8 7 6 5 4 3 2

Library of Congress Cataloging-in-Publication Data
Johannessen, Kristin Bergljot.
   Hooked on triangles : 19 quilts for foundation piecing / Kristin Bergljot Johannessen and Turid Margaret Uren.
      p. cm.
   ISBN 1-56477-546-1
   1. Patchwork—Patterns. 2. Quilting. 3. Triangle in art. I. Uren, Turid Margaret. II. Title.
   TT835.J5833 2004
   746.46'041—dc22
                                                2004010487

CONTENTS

INTRODUCTION

THIS STORY STARTED about 20 years ago. That was when we fell in love with patchwork and quilting, and it has since grown into a lifelong love affair.

From the very beginning, we were drawn to classic patchwork with basic rectangles, squares, and triangles. We soon mastered template-free shapes, but we found making triangle squares—squares pieced from two triangles—time consuming. With our busy lives, we welcomed every timesaving method introduced for triangle squares, and believe us, we tried them all!

Grids drawn directly on the fabric soon became our favorite method for sewing triangle squares, but we questioned whether we could streamline the process and make it even quicker. Why not draw the grids on paper? The grids could be photocopied as needed, laid on the fabrics, and stitched through, eliminating the need to draw the grid every time. We started experimenting and before long we had master grids in a lot of different sizes. We used the grids for all of our projects and handed them out to students whenever triangle squares were part of a class project.

The grids were so well received by our students and everyone else who used them that we decided to sell them. We started with five of the most popular metric sizes—2.5 cm, 5 cm, 7.5 cm, 10 cm, and 15 cm—but we soon added corresponding inch-size grids—1", 2", 3", 4", and 6". This combination of sizes can be mixed many ways to make blocks or quilts with more than one size of triangle squares.

We had to come up with a name for our product, and because we felt that there was a little magic involved in the fast and easy way that the triangle squares came together, we called it Magic with Triangles (MwT for short). In Norway, which is where we live, they are known as Tryll med Trekanter. As a result of this product, we registered our design company under the name "Tre Damer," which translates to "Three Ladies" in English. We are now selling Magic with Triangles on the Internet, along with our own line of patchwork patterns. To visit us, go to www.tredamer.no.

The more we use MwT, the more we see all the possibilities for easy piecing and template-free patchwork. Several sizes of triangle squares can be combined to make new and intriguing blocks or joined with rectangles and squares, making the design possibilities seem endless. We have to admit that we are "hooked on triangles"! And what is more natural than to share something you feel strongly about with others who have the same passion?

With this book, we hope to be an inspiration for those trying patchwork for the first time. We also hope to make piecing a little easier for the more experienced quilters. The projects are broken up into three sections. The quilts in the first section are made using only one size of triangle square per project. The second section gives quilts that use two sizes of triangle squares within each project. Quilts in the last section combine triangle squares with rectangles and squares. We hope there is something new and interesting for everyone.

ABOUT THE INSTRUCTIONS

THE PROJECTS IN this book were all made using the five triangle grids at the back of the book, identified by numbers 1–5. The larger the number, the larger the finished triangle square. Some projects are made using only one triangle-square size, so only one grid size will be used; others are made using more than one size of triangle square, so more than one grid will be used. To make it quick to see which size triangle-square grid(s) are required for each project, we have included this easy-to-read symbol at the beginning of the instructions. Each square marked with a red outline is a size used to make the featured quilt.

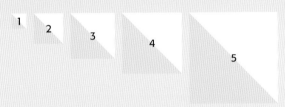

For a few of the projects, you can use any of the grids to yield a finished quilt in a size other than the one shown. However, some projects have fewer options or no other options than those given. Look for the options information that accompanies the projects; it will tell you what grid or grid combinations can be substituted. Yardage requirements and cutting instructions are based on the original quilt size, however, so if you do use a different grid, be aware that the yardage and cutting numbers will not be correct for any size other than the original. We offer helpful advice for changing block sizes and recalculating yardage amounts and the size of other pieces in "Making Changes" on page 8.

You also will notice that the instructions give two cutting methods for the triangle squares. Method 1 will instruct you to cut strips or pieces of fabric to use with the aforementioned grids. We obviously prefer this method but understand that everyone may not. Method 2 specifies the number and size of squares to cut from the appropriate fabrics to make triangle squares using another popular method. Detailed instructions for both methods are given in the next section, "Triangle-Square Construction."

TRIANGLE-SQUARE CONSTRUCTION

W E KNOW THAT there are many ways to construct triangle squares. We have tried them all, remember? You may think that you have already found your favorite method, but if you have never constructed triangles with paper grids, we urge you to give it a try. The instructions for method 1 explain how we do it. Of course, other methods for making triangle squares also can be used to make the quilts in this book. We offer method 2 as another option. Please be aware that if you choose to use method 2, the yardage amounts given for the blocks in the project materials sections may be more than you will require.

Method 1

1. Cut the number of strips or pieces from the appropriate fabrics as indicated in the project cutting instructions under method 1. If the instructions call for an assortment of fabrics or if you prefer a scrappier look, you may substitute pieces of fabric that are no smaller than the trimmed grids (see steps 2 and 3). You will need one piece of each of the two fabrics that appear in the finished triangle square. For example, if half of the finished triangle square is red and the other half is blue, you will need one piece *each* of red and blue.

2. Copy the grid(s) specified in the project instructions the number of times indicated. You'll find these grids at the back of the book. Always make copies from the original master grid. Never make copies from a copy!

Tip: Make your copies on the blank side of paper from your recycling bin.

3. Trim the excess paper ¼" from the grid outer line on each copy.

4. Refer to the project instructions to cut the fabric strips or pieces into pieces the same size as the trimmed grid, using the trimmed grid(s) as a template.

5. Place two of the appropriate fabric pieces right sides together. Pin a trimmed grid in the specified size to the top of the layered fabrics. Avoid pinning into the dotted lines.

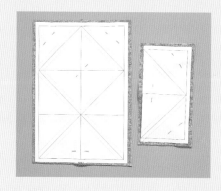

6

6. Set your sewing machine for 18 to 20 stitches per inch. Stitch through all of the layers along the grid dotted lines.

7. Remove the pins. Cut the grid apart on the solid lines with either a rotary cutter or scissors. Begin with the outer lines; then cut the piece into squares along the inner vertical and horizontal lines. Cut each square in half on the diagonal solid line to separate the triangle squares.

Note: To accurately cut apart the triangle squares, cut only one grid at a time. Do not layer the grids and cut them apart.

8. Gently remove the paper. The short stitch width perforates the paper, which should make it easy to remove. If you have problems, finger-press the paper triangle toward the seam allowance, and then tear it off.

9. The quilting Golden Rule is to iron seam allowances toward the darker half of the square, but from time to time the block construction may be easier if you press some seam allowances toward the lighter fabric. For 1" triangle squares, press the seam allowances open.

10. Trim the seam allowance points that extend beyond the squares.

Method 2

1. Cut the number of squares from the appropriate fabrics as indicated in the project cutting instructions under method 2.

2. Pair the squares indicated in the project instructions right sides together and draw a diagonal line on the lightest square in each pair. Pin the squares together along the marked line.

3. With the marked square on top, stitch ¼" from each side of the drawn line.

4. Cut the squares on the drawn line. Each pair of squares will yield two triangle squares.

5. The quilting Golden Rule is to iron seam allowances toward the darker half of the square, but from time to time the block construction may be easier if you press some seam allowances toward the lighter fabric. For the 1" triangle squares, press the seam allowances open.

6. Trim the seam allowance points that extend beyond the squares.

MAKING CHANGES

A S WE MENTIONED before, it is possible to make a different quilt size by using a grid size other than the one specified to make your triangle squares. Just refer to the options information for a suitable alternative, especially if more than one triangle-square size is used in the quilt. Of course, you also can increase or decrease the number of blocks used to change the finished quilt size. Any adjustments to the original quilt instructions will require changes in other areas as well.

If the triangle squares are used as the actual block, the only changes you may need to make if you use a different grid are in the yardage amounts, the border lengths, and possibly the border width. If the triangle squares are part of a block, and other pieces such as squares and rectangles are needed to complete the block, the sizes of the squares and rectangles will change along with the size of the triangle squares. With help from a few formulas, the changes are easily made.

Changing the Grid Size

To calculate new yardage requirements if you are making the triangle squares in a different size, refer to the chart below and the instructions that follow.

1. Choose the grid you want to use for your triangle squares.

2. Decide if you will be adding or deleting blocks from the original quilt size.

3. Determine the number of squares needed from each fabric color to make the triangle squares. Remember that each triangle square requires one square of *each* of the two fabric colors that it is made of. Each pair of squares will yield two triangle squares.

4. Refer to the chart to see how many triangle squares you can get from each grid. Make as many copies of the grid as needed to yield enough triangle squares for your project.

5. Look at the chart to see how many trimmed grids will fit on each strip of fabric. Determine the amount of strips needed. You will need this many strips from *each* of the two fabric colors.

6. The last column in the chart gives the width to cut the strips. Multiply the width by the number of strips needed to determine the yardage required from each fabric for the triangle squares.

Grid Number (Finished Size)	Number of Triangle Squares Yielded per Grid	Number of Grids That Will Fit on Each Fabric Strip	Width to Cut Fabric Strip
1 (1")	30	4	7"
2 (2")	12	4	7"
3 (3")	4	4	5"
4 (4")	4	3	6"
5 (6")	2	5	8"

Changing the Size of Other Pieces in a Block

If your triangle squares are part of a block that is also made up of squares and/or rectangles, any changes made to the size of the triangle squares will affect the size of those pieces. Below are two examples to show you how simple it is to calculate the new measurements.

To calculate the yardage required for the new pieces, you can use a system similar to that used to calculate yardage when using a different size grid (refer to "Changing the Grid Size" on page 8). Figure out how wide the strips will need to be cut for those pieces and how many strips you need from each color for the whole project. Multiply the width by the number of strips to determine the yardage required.

Calculating New Block Measurements: Example 1

Here is the block we want to change to a new size:

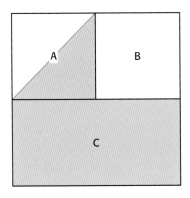

1. Start by choosing the size of unit A, the triangle square. For this project, we want to use grid 3. We know that the *finished* size of the triangle square is 3" x 3". That means that the triangle square with seam allowances is 3½" x 3½" (3" + ¼" seam allowance on each side).

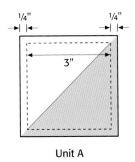

Unit A

2. In this block, unit B is the same size as unit A, so it needs to be cut 3½" x 3½".

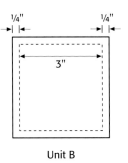

Unit B

3. Join unit A to unit B. By sewing them together you lose the seam allowance from one side of each of the pieces in the seam. Unit AB now measures 3½" x 6½" (finished size of unit A + finished size of unit B + seam allowances on each side).

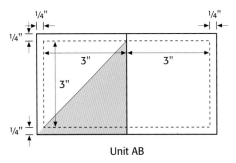

Unit AB

Master of the Block

If you remember these calculation rules, you will soon be "Master of the Block" and be able to make blocks in whatever size you want to fit the size of your project.

• Start with the size of the triangle square, including seam allowances.
• Remember to add seam allowances to all four sides of every piece.
• The seam allowances are lost after sewing the pieces together.

4. Unit C is equal to unit AB. Cut unit C so that it measures 3½" x 6½".

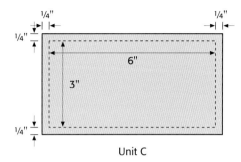

Unit C

5. Sew the units together. With seam allowances, the block will measure 6½" x 6½". When the block is incorporated into the quilt, all of the seam allowances will be lost, resulting in a finished block that measures 6" x 6".

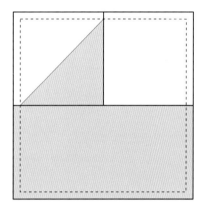

Finished Block: 6" x 6"

Calculating New Block Measurements: Example 2

For this example, we will use a block from "Monkey Wrench?" (page 83).

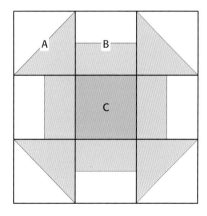

1. We want our block to be smaller than the one used in the project, and we want to use grid 2 for unit A, the triangle square. The *finished* size of the triangle square is 2" x 2". With seam allowances, the triangle square is 2½" x 2½" (2" + ¼" seam allowance on each side).

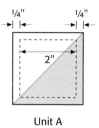

Unit A

2. Unit B is a pieced square that finishes to the same size as the triangle square, 2" x 2". The square is divided in half equally, so each strip is 1" x 2" *finished*. With seam allowances, the strips must be cut 1½" x 2½".

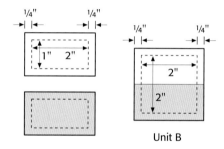

Unit B

3. Unit C is also the same finished size as unit A. Cut unit C squares 2½" x 2½".

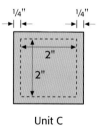

Unit C

4. Now join all the pieces to make the block. Because each unit has a finished size of 2", the block finished size is 6" x 6". If you include seam allowances, it's 6½" x 6½".

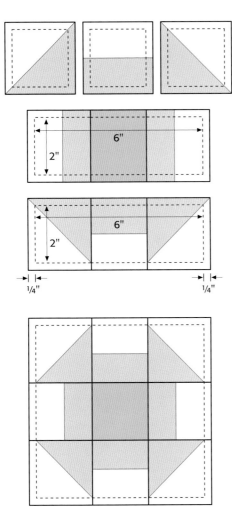

Finished Block: 6" x 6"

Calculating New Borders and Binding

To determine new yardage for borders and binding, we recommend that you first make the pieced quilt center. The following steps describe the calculation process.

1. Decide how wide you want your borders to be.

2. Measure the quilt-top length and multiply the number by 2. Repeat with the quilt-top width. Add the measurements to see how many total inches of border strips you will need. Divide the number by 40 (the amount of usable inches per strip). Round up to the nearest whole number to determine how many strips you will need. Multiply the border width by the number of strips needed, and you have your new yardage for borders.

Note: If your borders are longer than the fabric width and will need to be pieced to achieve the required length, you will need to estimate where the seam will fall on the quilt top. Because you do not want a seam near the ends of the border strip, it may be necessary to add an additional length to the border strip so that you can position the seam elsewhere.

3. For binding, assemble the quilt top and borders. Measure the quilt perimeter to see how many inches of binding you will need. Add an additional 10" to allow for turning and mitered corners. Divide the number by 40 (the amount of usable inches per strip) to determine how many strips you will need. We cut our binding strips 2½" wide. Multiply the binding width by the number of strips needed and you have your new yardage for binding.

BASIC QUILTING TECHNIQUES

I N THIS SECTION we review the basic instructions required for constructing your quilt. Refer to "Finishing Instructions" on page 15 for techniques on completing your quilt once the top is finished.

Rotary Cutting

The rotary-cutting method is used throughout this book for cutting all of the pieces needed to make the projects. All cutting measurements include ¼"-wide seam allowances. You will need a cutting mat, a square ruler, a long ruler, and a cutter with a sharp blade. For those unfamiliar with rotary cutting, refer to the following instructions.

1. Straighten one cut edge of your fabric. To do this, fold the fabric in half, selvage to selvage, aligning the lengthwise grain as much as possible. Place the folded edge closest to you on the cutting mat. Align one edge of a square ruler along the folded edge, placing the ruler far enough from the left edge to ensure that the first cut will go through both layers of fabric. Place a long, straight ruler along the left side of the square ruler. Make sure the angle is right before you remove the square ruler.

Make your first cut along the right side of the long ruler and discard the strip.

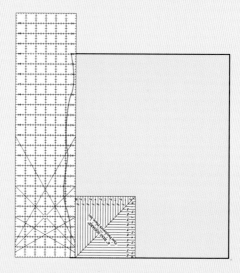

2. To cut strips, align the required measurement mark on the ruler with the straight edge of the fabric. Cut as many strips as needed for your project.

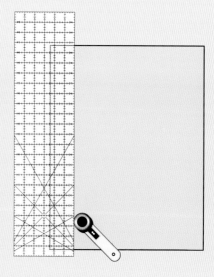

3. To cut squares from the strips, align the correct mark on the ruler, which will be the same as the strip width, and cut the strip crosswise.

Achieving Accurate Seam Allowances

All seam allowances for the projects in this book are ¼" wide and are included in the cutting measurements. The easiest way to ensure that your seam allowances are consistent is to use a special presser foot that measures exactly ¼" from the needle center position to the edge of the presser foot. Align the cut edges of the pieces you are sewing with the edge of the presser foot when stitching.

If a ¼" presser foot is not available for your sewing machine, adhere masking tape to the throat plate on the machine, ¼" away from the needle. To find the right placement, use the seam allowance from one of the triangle grids. Cut out one triangle, place the piece under the presser foot, and insert the needle through the dotted line. Place a piece of tape along the solid line.

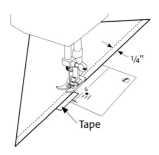

Assembling the Quilt Top

Blocks can be arranged in either a straight setting or a diagonal setting. For both settings, the blocks are first stitched together into rows and then the rows are stitched together.

To assemble a straight setting, refer to the project instructions to arrange the blocks into horizontal rows. Make an effort to match the seams between blocks.

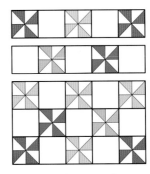

Straight-Set Quilt

To assemble a diagonal setting, arrange your blocks in diagonal rows, adding the side setting triangles to the ends of the rows. Stitch the corner triangles to the quilt top last. Again, make an effort to match the seams between blocks.

Diagonally Set Quilt

Adding Borders

Do not underestimate the importance of borders. Borders can "make or break" a quilt. When it comes to making a decision on borders, there are many things to take into consideration: the number of borders, the width of the borders, and the color of each border.

If you are working on a large quilt with sides that are longer than the standard width of most fabrics, you have two choices. You can either cut strips the width of the fabric and sew them together to make a strip long enough to fit, or you can purchase enough fabric to cut a strip the desired measurement along the length of the fabric. Piecing is usually more economical, but if you opt for lengthwise-cut strips, it is a good way to build up your stash!

The cutting instructions for the quilts in this book instruct you to cut the required number of strips across the width of the fabric. You will then need to measure the quilt top to determine the exact length of the borders. To measure the quilt top for borders, follow these steps:

1. Measure the quilt top through the center from side to side. Cut two border strips to that measurement, piecing and trimming the strips as needed to achieve the required length. Mark the center of the quilt's top and bottom edges and the center edge of each border strip. Pin the strips to the top and bottom edges, beginning at the center marks and matching the ends. Sew the borders to the quilt top. Press the seams toward the borders.

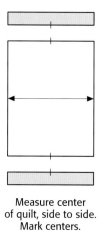

Measure center
of quilt, side to side.
Mark centers.

2. Measure the length of the quilt top from top to bottom, including the top and bottom borders just added. Cut two border strips to that measurement, piecing and trimming the strips as needed to achieve the required length. Mark the center of each side of the quilt top and the center edge of each border strip. Pin the strips to the sides, beginning at the center marks and matching the ends. Sew the borders to the quilt top. Press the seams toward the borders.

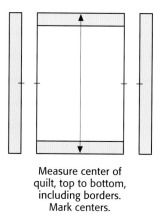

Measure center of
quilt, top to bottom,
including borders.
Mark centers.

3. Repeat steps 1 and 2 for any additional borders.

FINISHING INSTRUCTIONS

You may have heard it before: It's not a quilt until it's quilted! Whether you decide to finish the quilt by hand or machine, this section will take you through the steps needed to finish your quilt so that you and others can enjoy it.

Marking the Quilting Lines

Marking before or after the quilt top is layered and basted together with the batting and backing depends on the quilting design. If you are quilting in the ditch, outline quilting, or free-motion quilting, the quilt does not need to be marked before layering. If you are quilting a simple shape or using a quilting stencil to mark the design, you can mark the top either before or after basting. However, if you are quilting a more intricate design, mark the quilt top before layering.

Cutting the Backing

Measure the finished quilt top. Cut the backing at least 4" larger than the quilt top on all sides. For large quilts, it is usually necessary to sew two or more lengths of fabric together to make a piece large enough for the backing. The most common ways to sew the lengths together are shown above right. You can choose to either seam the pieces through the middle, or cut one of the lengths in half lengthwise and stitch one half to each side of the full-width piece. Occasionally it is more economical to piece the lengths crosswise. We have indicated the

piecing direction after the yardage amounts in the materials section. The piecing direction is not indicated for square quilts.

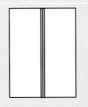

Two lengths of fabric seamed in the center   Partial fabric width

From time to time we realize that the fabric we have selected for the backing is just a few inches too small or the size of the quilt top is so close to the standard width of fabric that it seems a waste of money to buy another length to make a large enough piece. Our way of solving these problems is to make a pieced backing, which usually makes the project more interesting. For instance, the main backing fabric for "Down the Road" (page 70) wasn't large enough until some simple borders were added.

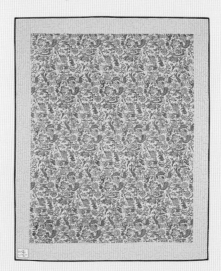

Not enough fabric was purchased for the backing of "Through the Maze" (page 53), but by the insertion of a few leftover triangle squares, the problem was soon solved. You can see how pieced backings add unexpected interest and keep the scrap bag from overflowing!

Layering and Basting the Quilt

Now it's time to make the quilt "sandwich," which consists of layering and basting the quilt top, batting, and backing.

1. Spread the backing wrong side up on a flat surface. If possible, hold it in place with masking tape or pins, depending on the surface. Be careful not to stretch the backing out of shape.

2. Layer the batting over the backing. Cut it slightly smaller than the backing.

3. Place the pressed quilt top right side up over the batting. Position the quilt top so that the edges of the top are parallel with the edges of the backing. Pin it in place with a few pins, avoiding any areas you plan to baste.

4. Beginning at the center, baste diagonally from corner to corner. Continue basting a grid of lines both vertically and horizontally, about 6"

apart. Finish by basting around the edges. To avoid fraying the edges of the quilt top, it is a good idea to fold the backing just over the edges of the quilt top and baste through all the layers. (Be careful not to fold the backing so far over the borders that it interferes with the quilting design.) Then, when you have done all your quilting, just remove the basting and the edge of the border will appear as fresh and sharp as when it was cut!

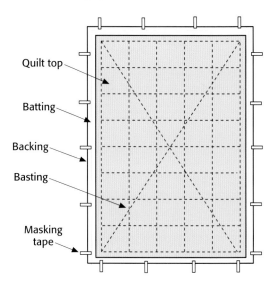

Quilting

You can quilt your project by hand or machine; select the method you prefer. Basic instructions are included below for both. To get a quilt with flat, straight borders, quilt the borders with the same density as the rest of the quilt.

Hand Quilting

To quilt by hand, you will need quilting needles called Betweens, quilting thread, and a thimble. A frame or hoop is also helpful for supporting your work.

1. Thread your needle with a single strand of quilting thread about 18" long. Make a small knot at the end of the thread.

2. Decide where you want to start your quilting. Insert the needle through the top and batting, about 1" from the place where you will make your first stitch; pull it out at the point where

you want to start. Pull slightly on the thread to make the knot pop under the surface and fasten into the batting; backstitch.

3. Take small, evenly spaced running stitches through all of the quilt layers until the thread is used up or you want to start in a different place.

4. To end, take a small backstitch and bring the needle to the top about one stitch length in front of the backstitch. Make a small knot in the thread, about ¼" from the quilt-top surface. Then insert the needle into the quilt sandwich again, surfacing about a needle's length away. Pull on the thread and pop the knot into the batting. Clip the thread at the surface.

Machine Quilting

Over the last few years, machine quilting has become more and more accepted, even among the most serious of quiltmakers. You can either do the quilting on your own sewing machine or have someone with a long-arm machine do the quilting for you. If you decide to do the quilting yourself, you will need a darning foot for all free-motion quilting; a walking foot is highly recommended for all straight-line quilting. There are already a multitude of excellent books on this subject, so instead of going into a thorough explanation, we recommend that you study one of those books.

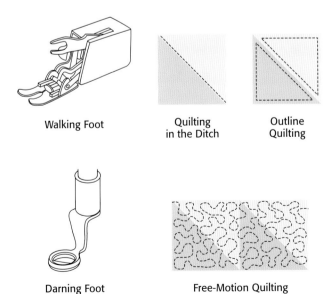

Walking Foot

Quilting in the Ditch

Outline Quilting

Darning Foot

Free-Motion Quilting

If you decide to free-motion quilt, take some time to read the instructions for your machine regarding working with a darning foot. Make a lot of samples to get familiar with the motion and speed of both the machine and your hands. The best results are accomplished with a combination of a lot of practice and a little artistic sense.

Trimming and Straightening the Quilt

Trim the backing and batting even with the quilt top. Remember that due to shrinkage caused by the quilting, the quilt is now smaller than the measurements of the original quilt top. The two corresponding sides should measure the same. Square up the quilt if necessary. You can make small adjustments when you attach the binding.

Adding a Hanging Sleeve

If you plan to display your quilt on a wall, add a hanging sleeve to the quilt backing to hold the rod.

1. From leftover backing fabric or a matching fabric, cut a strip 5" wide and 1" shorter than the width of the quilt. Make a double-folded hem at each end and press the strip in half lengthwise, wrong sides together.

2. Align the raw edges of the folded strip with the top edge of the quilt backing; pin or baste the strip in place. Follow the instructions in "Binding" on page 18 to secure the raw edges.

Baste sleeve to top edge of quilt.

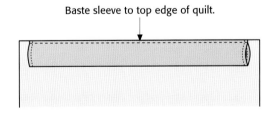

3. After the binding has been attached, blindstitch the folded edge of the sleeve to the backing.

Binding

All the quilts in this book have been bound with a double-folded binding. We find that this type of binding is easy to attach and very durable.

1. Start by cutting the number of strips indicated in the project instructions. Cut each strip 2½" wide across the width of the fabric. Join the strips at right angles, right sides together, to make one continuous strip. Trim the seam allowances to ¼" and press them open.

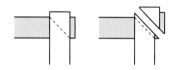

Joining Straight-Cut Strips

2. Trim the beginning of the strip at a 45° angle. Press the angled edge under ¼". Press the strip in half lengthwise, wrong sides together.

Fold line

3. Place the angled end on the quilt top at the center of the bottom edge, aligning the raw edges. Stitch the binding to the bottom edge of the quilt, using a ¼" seam allowance. End the stitching ¼" from the corner of the quilt; backstitch. Remove the quilt from under the needle.

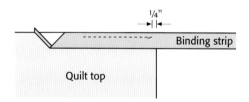

¼"

Binding strip

Quilt top

4. Fold the binding up, away from the quilt, at a 45° angle. Then fold the binding back down again so that it is parallel with the edge of the quilt. Pin the fold in place.

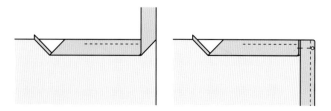

5. Pin the binding to the quilt top the length of the side to be stitched. Stitch the binding in place, ending ¼" before the next corner; backstitch and repeat step 5. Repeat the stitching and folding process for all of the remaining edges and corners.

6. As you approach the point where you began, stop with the needle down in the binding. Overlap the ends of the binding strip. Leave about 1" of overlap and cut away the excess, trimming the end at a 45° angle. Tuck the end inside the fold at the beginning of the strip. Continue stitching the binding in place.

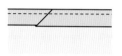

7. Fold the binding over the raw edges of the quilt to the back, making sure the folded edge covers the machine stitching. Blindstitch the binding in place. A miter will form at each corner. Blindstitch the mitered corners in place.

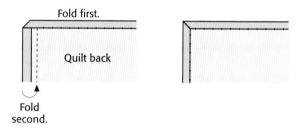

Fold first.

Quilt back

Fold
second.

Signing Your Quilt

Be sure to sign and date your quilts. If the quilt is a gift, a personalized label will make the gift so much more special for the lucky recipient. Even if the quilt is made for no special occasion, future generations of quilt lovers will thank you for giving them this valuable information.

One-Triangle-Square Wonders

Quilts Made with a
Single Triangle-Square Size

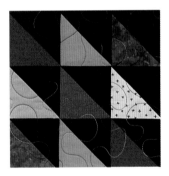

Back to Basics

Rhinestones

Multitriangles I

Multitriangles II

Blue Stars

Back to Basics

By Turid Margaret Uren. Machine quilted by AKD Quilteteknikk.

"Back to Basics" is a one-block scrap quilt made completely of triangle squares. One half of each block is dark blue and the other half is a bright-color fabric. The outer-border fabric inspired my choice of fabrics for the triangle squares. This project is so easy to make that we recommend it for first-time quilters.—Turid

FINISHED QUILT SIZE: 52½" x 76½"
FINISHED BLOCK SIZE: 4" x 4"

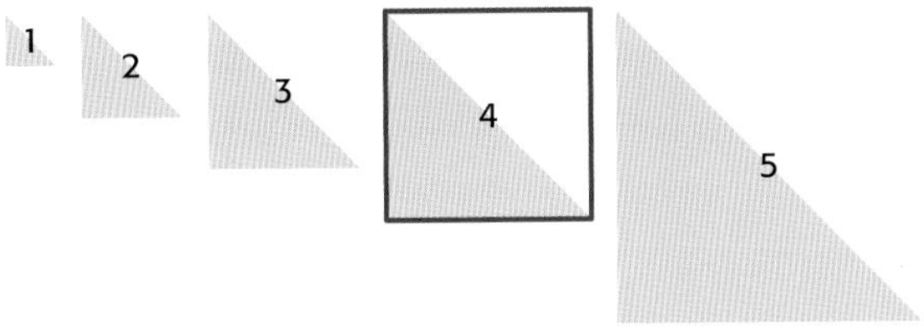

OPTIONS: The blocks can be made in five different sizes with any of the grids given at the back of the book. Finished block sizes are given below for each grid size.

Grid	Finished Block Size
1	1" x 1"
2	2" x 2"
3	3" x 3"
4	4" x 4"
5	6" x 6"

Materials

Yardage is calculated for grid 4 using method 1 and is based on 42"-wide fabric. Refer to "Making Changes" on page 8 to recalculate yardage if you use a grid size other than grid 4.

- ▲ 3⅛ yards of dark blue solid for blocks and inner border
- ▲ 2⅝ yards *total* of assorted brights for blocks
- ▲ 1⅛ yards of multicolor print for outer border
- ▲ ⅝ yard of fabric for binding
- ▲ 5 yards of fabric for backing (lengthwise seam)
- ▲ 56" x 80" piece of batting

Cutting for Triangle Squares

All measurements include ¼"-wide seam allowances.

Fabrics	For method 1, cut:	For method 2, cut:
Dark blue solid	14 strips, 6" x 42"	80 squares, 4⅞" x 4⅞"
Assorted brights	14 strips, 6" x 42"; or 40 pieces no smaller than 5⅜" x 10¼"	80 squares, 4⅞" x 4⅞"

Cutting for Remaining Pieces

All measurements include ¼"-wide seam allowances.

Fabrics	Size to Cut
Dark blue solid	7 strips, 2½" x 42"
Multicolor print	7 strips, 4½" x 42"
Binding fabric	7 strips, 2½" x 42"

Making the Triangle Squares

Make 160 triangle squares that are half dark blue and half bright, following the instructions below for the desired method.

Method 1: Refer to the instructions on page 6 to make and trim 40 copies of grid 4. Cut the dark blue 6" x 42" strips into 40 rectangles; use the trimmed grids as a guide. If you have cut strips from the assorted bright fabrics, use the trimmed grids to cut 40 rectangles. If you are using pieces of assorted bright fabrics, cut them to the same size as the grids if necessary; use the trimmed grids as a guide.

Pair each dark blue rectangle with an assorted bright rectangle. Make the triangle squares.

Method 2: Refer to the instructions on page 7 to pair each dark blue square with an assorted bright square. Make the triangle squares.

Make 160.

Assembling the Quilt Top

1. Refer to the quilt assembly diagram to arrange the blocks into 16 rows of 10 blocks each. Take time to spread out the colors evenly and make sure all of the blocks are oriented so that the dark blue triangle is in the right half of the block. Stitch the blocks in each row together, and then stitch the rows together.

2. Refer to "Adding Borders" on page 14 to join and trim the dark blue 2½" x 42" strips as needed to make inner borders of the correct length. Stitch the inner top and bottom borders to the quilt top first, and then add the inner side borders. Repeat with the multicolor outer-border strips.

Quilt Assembly Diagram

Finishing

Refer to "Finishing Instructions" on pages 15–18.

1. Layer the quilt top with batting and backing; baste.

2. Quilt as desired.

3. Add a hanging sleeve, if desired.

4. Bind the edges and add a label.

Rhinestones

By Turid Margaret Uren. Machine quilted by AKD Quilteteknikk.

*This project has all the qualities a quilter finds appealing: it's easy, it's fun, and it's quick!
And if you have an abundance of scraps, this bright and cheerful quilt is a
great way to help deplete the stack.*—TURID

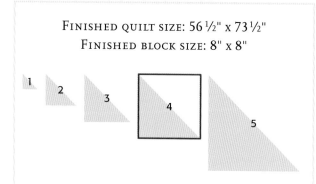

FINISHED QUILT SIZE: 56½" x 73½"
FINISHED BLOCK SIZE: 8" x 8"

OPTIONS: The blocks can be made in five different sizes with any of the grids given at the back of the book. Finished block sizes are given below for each grid size.

Grid	Finished Block Size
1	2" x 2"
2	4" x 4"
3	6" x 6"
4	8" x 8"
5	12" x 12"

Materials

Yardage is calculated for grid 4 using method 1 and is based on 42"-wide fabric. Refer to "Making Changes" on page 8 to recalculate yardage if you use a grid size other than grid 4.

- ▲ 2½ yards *total* of assorted whites and/or tans for blocks
- ▲ 1¼ yards of medium blue solid for outer border
- ▲ ⅞ yard *total* of assorted greens for blocks
- ▲ ¾ yard of dark blue solid for sashing and inner border
- ▲ ⅝ yard *each* of assorted reds, yellows, and blues for blocks
- ▲ ½ yard of red solid for middle border
- ▲ ⅝ yard of fabric for binding
- ▲ 4 yards of fabric for backing (crosswise seam)
- ▲ 61" x 78" piece of batting

Cutting for Triangle Squares

All measurements include ¼"-wide seam allowances.

Fabrics	For method 1, cut:	For method 2, cut:
Assorted whites and/or tans	12 strips, 6" x 42"; or 35 pieces no smaller than 5⅜" x 10¼"	70 squares, 4⅞" x 4⅞"
Assorted reds	3 strips, 6" x 42"; or 9 pieces no smaller than 5⅜" x 10¼"	18 squares, 4⅞" x 4⅞"
Assorted yellows	3 strips, 6" x 42"; or 7 pieces no smaller than 5⅜" x 10¼"	14 squares, 4⅞" x 4⅞"
Assorted blues	3 strips, 6" x 42"; or 8 pieces no smaller than 5⅜" x 10¼"	16 squares, 4⅞" x 4⅞"
Assorted greens	4 strips, 6" x 42"; or 11 pieces no smaller than 5⅜" x 10¼"	22 squares, 4⅞" x 4⅞"

Cutting for Remaining Pieces

All measurements include ¼"-wide seam allowances.

Fabrics	Size to Cut
Dark blue solid	20 strips, 1" x 42; crosscut 7 strips into 28 strips, 1" x 8½"
Red solid	6 strips, 2" x 42"
Medium blue solid	7 strips, 5½" x 42"
Binding fabric	7 strips, 2½" x 42"

Making the Triangle Squares and Blocks

1. Make the number of each triangle-square color combination shown, following the instructions below for the desired method.

    Method 1: Refer to the instructions on page 6 to make and trim 35 copies of grid 4. If you have cut strips from the block fabrics, use the trimmed grids to cut 35 assorted white and/or tan rectangles, 9 assorted red rectangles, 7 assorted yellow rectangles, 8 assorted blue rectangles, and 11 assorted green rectangles. If you are using pieces of fabric, cut them to the same size as the grids if necessary; use the trimmed grids as a guide.

    Pair an assorted white and/or tan rectangle with each assorted red, yellow, blue, and green rectangle. Make the triangle squares.

    Method 2: Refer to the instructions on page 7 to pair an assorted white and/or tan 4⅞" square with each assorted red, yellow, blue, and green 4⅞" square. Make the triangle squares.

Make 36.

Make 28.

Make 32.

Make 44.

2. Join four triangle squares from the same color family as shown. Make the number of blocks shown for each color combination.

Make 9.

Make 7.

Make 8.

Make 11.

Assembling the Quilt Top

1. Arrange the blocks into seven rows of five blocks each.

2. Stitch a dark blue 1" x 8½" vertical sashing strip between the blocks in each row as shown.

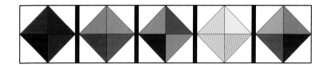

3. Join and trim the remaining dark blue 1" x 42" strips as needed to make eight strips, 1" x 42½", and two strips, 1" x 60½". Refer to the quilt assembly diagram on page 26 to alternately stitch the 1" x 42½" strips and block rows together as shown. Stitch the 1" x 60½" strips to each side of the quilt top.

4. Refer to "Adding Borders" on page 14 to join and trim the red solid strips as needed to make middle borders of the correct length. Stitch the middle top and bottom borders to the quilt top first, and then add the middle side borders. Repeat with the medium blue outer-border strips.

Quilt Assembly Diagram

"Blue Rhinestones"
by Kristin Bergljot Johannessen, 24" x 28".

A two-color quilt can create just as much excitement as one with many colors. This variation of "Rhinestones" was made using grid 2 triangle squares.

Finishing

Refer to "Finishing Instructions" on pages 15–18.

1. Layer the quilt top with batting and backing; baste.

2. Quilt as desired.

3. Add a hanging sleeve, if desired.

4. Bind the edges and add a label.

Multitriangles I

By Turid Margaret Uren

*We just love scrap quilts, and with a block like this that uses many triangles,
you can really put your scraps to work. This quilt is made primarily from a lot of
different red prints with a few purples thrown in for fun and excitement.
Take the challenge with your scrap pile and make something wild!*—TURID

FINISHED QUILT SIZE: 44½" x 44½"
FINISHED BLOCK SIZE: 12" x 12"

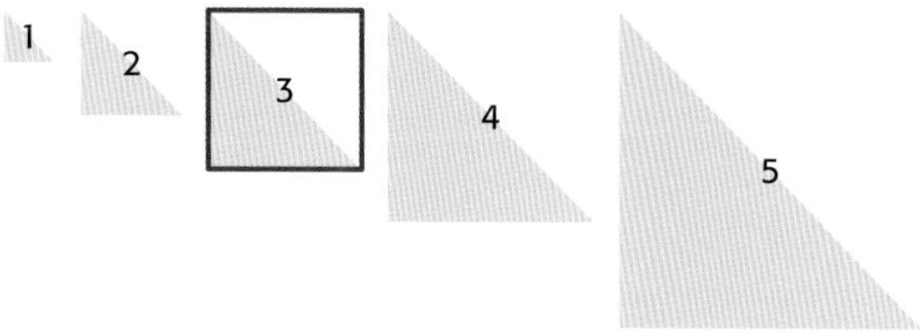

OPTIONS: The blocks can be made in five different sizes with any of the grids given at the back of the book. Finished block sizes are given below for each grid size.

Grid	Finished Block Size
1	4" x 4"
2	8" x 8"
3	12" x 12"
4	16" x 16"
5	24" x 24"

Materials

Yardage is calculated for grid 3 using method 1 and is based on 42"-wide fabric. Refer to "Making Changes" on page 8 to recalculate yardage if you use a grid size other than grid 3.

▲ 1½ yards *total* of assorted whites and/or tans for blocks
▲ 1½ yards *total* of assorted reds and/or purples for blocks
▲ ⅝ yard of dark red print for outer border
▲ ¼ yard of red solid for inner border
▲ ½ yard of fabric for binding
▲ 3½ yards of fabric for backing
▲ 49" x 49" piece of batting

Cutting for Triangle Squares

All measurements include ¼"-wide seam allowances.

Fabrics	For method 1, cut:	For method 2, cut:
Assorted reds and/or purples	9 strips, 5" x 42"; or 36 pieces no smaller than 4⅜" x 8¼"	72 squares, 3⅞" x 3⅞"
Assorted whites and/or tans	9 strips, 5" x 42"; or 36 pieces no smaller than 4⅜" x 8¼"	72 squares, 3⅞" x 3⅞"

Cutting for Remaining Pieces

All measurements include ¼"-wide seam allowances.

Fabrics	Size to Cut
Red solid	4 strips, 1½" x 42"
Dark red print	5 strips, 3½" x 42"
Binding fabric	5 strips, 2½" x 42"

Making the Triangle Squares and Blocks

1. Make the number of each triangle-square color combination shown, following the instructions below for the desired method.

   Method 1: Refer to the instructions on page 6 to make and trim 36 copies of grid 3. If you have cut strips from the fabrics, use the trimmed grids to cut 36 rectangles from the assorted red and/or purple strips and 36 rectangles from the assorted white and/or tan strips. If you are using pieces of fabric, cut them to the same size as the grids if necessary; use the trimmed grids as a guide.

   Pair 18 assorted red and/or purple rectangles with assorted white and/or tan rectangles. Pair 9 assorted white and/or tan rectangles with 9 different assorted white and/or tan rectangles. Pair 9 assorted red and/or purple rectangles with 9 different assorted red and/or purple rectangles. Make the triangle squares.

   Method 2: Refer to the instructions on page 7 to pair 36 assorted red and/or purple squares with assorted white and/or tan squares. Pair 18 assorted white and/or tan squares with 18 different assorted white and/or tan squares. Pair 18 assorted red and/or purple squares with 18 different assorted red and/or purple squares. Make the triangle squares.

Make 72.   Make 36.   Make 36.

2. Arrange the triangle squares as shown to make the Multitriangles block. Make nine.

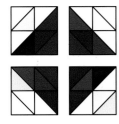 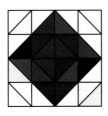

Make 9.

Assembling the Quilt Top

1. Arrange the blocks into three rows of three blocks each. Stitch the blocks in each row together, and then stitch the rows together.

2. Refer to "Adding Borders" on page 14 to trim the red solid strips as needed to make inner borders of the correct length. Stitch the inner top and bottom borders to the quilt top first, and then add the inner side borders. Join and trim the dark red print strips as needed to make outer-border strips of the correct length. Stitch the outer top and bottom borders to the quilt top first, and then add the outer side borders.

Quilt Assembly Diagram

Finishing

Refer to "Finishing Instructions" on pages 15–18.

1. Layer the quilt top with batting and backing; baste.

2. Quilt as desired.

3. Add a hanging sleeve, if desired.

4. Bind the edges and add a label.

Multitriangles II

By Turid Margaret Uren. Machine quilted by AKD Quilteteknikk.

*This is a tribute to Mother Nature, with her variety of earthy colors: green is for vegetation,
brown is for the soil that nurtures the roots, and the lightest colors represent the sky above.
It was a fun project to work with, and I challenged myself to use a lot of the scraps
that I normally have a hard time trying to fit into my projects. A good contrast
between the light and dark fabrics is important.*—TURID

FINISHED QUILT SIZE: 71½" x 83½"
FINISHED BLOCK SIZE: 12" x 12"

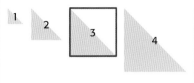

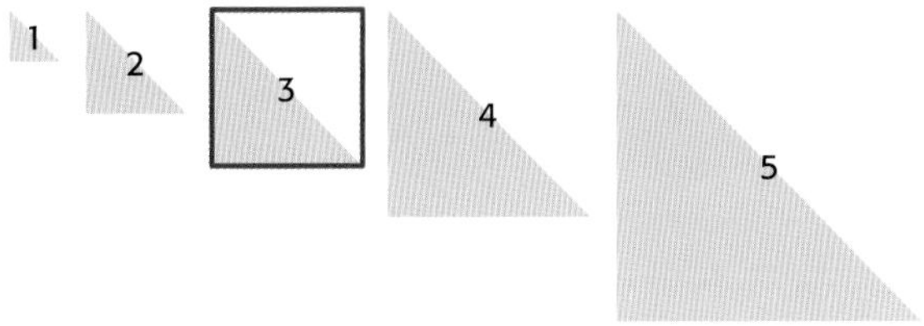

OPTIONS: The blocks can be made in five different sizes with any of the grids given at the back of the book. Finished block sizes are given below for each grid size.

Grid	Finished Block Size
1	4" x 4"
2	8" x 8"
3	12" x 12"
4	16" x 16"
5	24" x 24"

Materials

Yardage is calculated for grid 3 using method 1 and is based on 42"-wide fabric. Refer to "Making Changes" on page 8 to recalculate yardage if you use a grid size other than grid 3.

▲ 4¾ yards *total* of assorted lights (including light mint green) for blocks

▲ 2⅜ yards *total* of assorted medium to dark greens for blocks

▲ 2⅜ yards *total* of assorted medium to dark browns for blocks

▲ 1⅛ yards of medium green print for outer border

▲ ½ yard of dark green solid for inner border

▲ ¾ yard of fabric for binding

▲ 5 yards of fabric for backing (lengthwise seam)

▲ 76" x 88" piece of batting

Cutting for Triangle Squares

All measurements include ¼"-wide seam allowances.

Fabrics	For method 1, cut:	For method 2, cut:
Assorted lights	30 strips, 5" x 42"; or 120 pieces no smaller than 4⅜" x 8¼"	240 squares, 3⅞" x 3⅞"
Assorted greens	15 strips, 5" x 42"; or 60 pieces no smaller than 4⅜" x 8¼"	120 squares, 3⅞" x 3⅞"
Assorted browns	15 strips, 5" x 42"; or 60 pieces no smaller than 4⅜" x 8¼"	120 squares, 3⅞" x 3⅞"

Cutting for Remaining Pieces

All measurements include ¼"-wide seam allowances.

Fabrics	Size to Cut
Dark green solid	7 strips, 2" x 42"
Medium green print	8 strips, 4½" x 42"
Binding fabric	8 strips, 2½" x 42"

Making the Triangle Squares and Blocks

1. Make 240 triangle squares that are half light and half green and 240 triangle squares that are half light and half brown, following the instructions below for the desired method.

   Method 1: Refer to the instructions on page 6 to make and trim 120 copies of grid 3. If you have cut strips from the fabrics, use the trimmed grids to cut 120 rectangles from the assorted light strips and 60 rectangles *each* from the assorted green and brown strips. If you are using pieces of fabric, cut them to the same size as the grids if necessary; use the trimmed grids as a guide.

      Pair a light rectangle with each of the assorted green and brown rectangles. Make the triangle squares.

   Method 2: Refer to the instructions on page 7 to pair each of the assorted green and brown squares with a light square. Make the triangle squares.

Make 240.   Make 240.

2. Arrange 16 half-light-and-half-green triangle squares as shown to make the Multitriangles block. Make 15. Repeat with the half-light-and-half-brown triangle squares. Make 15.

Make 15.   Make 15.

Assembling the Quilt Top

1. Refer to the quilt assembly diagram to arrange the blocks into six horizontal rows of five blocks each. Stitch the blocks in each row together, and then stitch the rows together.

2. Refer to "Adding Borders" on page 14 to join and trim the dark green strips to make inner borders of the correct length. Stitch the top and bottom borders to the quilt top first, and then add the side borders. Repeat with the medium green outer-border strips.

Quilt Assembly Diagram

Finishing

Refer to "Finishing Instructions" on pages 15–18.

1. Layer the quilt top with batting and backing; baste.

2. Quilt as desired.

3. Add a hanging sleeve, if desired.

4. Bind the edges and add a label.

Blue Stars

By Kristin Bergljot Johannessen. Machine quilted by AKD Quilteteknikk.

*The ever-popular Star block and a king-sized pile of blue scraps were the inspiration for this quilt.
The project was so fun, and the triangle units so easy and fast to make, that it was hard
to stop making blocks. I didn't stop until I almost ran out of blue scraps!*—KRISTIN

FINISHED QUILT SIZE: 86½" x 98½"
FINISHED BLOCK SIZE: 12" x 12"

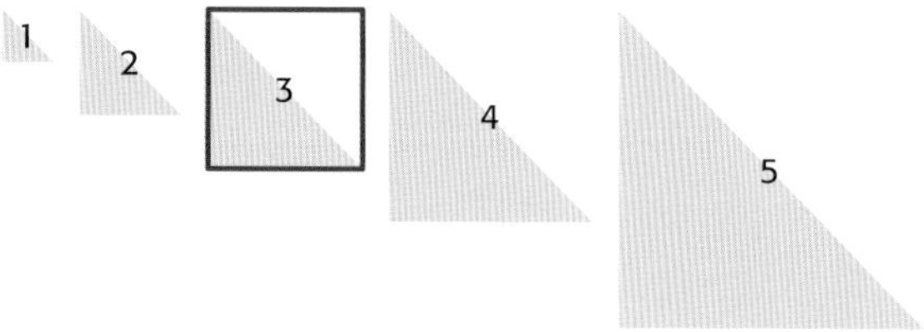

Materials

Yardage is calculated for grid 3 using method 1 and is based on 42"-wide fabric. Refer to "Making Changes" on page 8 to recalculate yardage if you use a grid size other than grid 3.

▲ 8 yards *total* of assorted medium and dark blues for blocks
▲ 5 yards *total* of assorted lights (including light blue) for blocks
▲ 2⅛ yards of dark blue for border
▲ ⅞ yard of fabric for binding
▲ 8 yards of fabric for backing (crosswise seams)
▲ 91" x 103" piece of batting

OPTIONS: The blocks can be made in five different sizes with any of the grids given at the back of the book. Finished block sizes are given below for each grid size.

Grid	Finished Block Size
1	4" x 4"
2	8" x 8"
3	12" x 12"
4	16" x 16"
5	24" x 24"

Cutting for Triangle Squares

All measurements include ¼"-wide seam allowances.

Fabrics	For method 1, cut:	For method 2, cut:
Assorted lights	32 strips, 5" x 42"; or 126 pieces no smaller than 4⅜" x 8¼"	252 squares, 3⅞" x 3⅞"
Assorted medium and dark blues	53 strips, 5" x 42"; or 210 pieces no smaller than 4⅜" x 8¼"	420 squares, 3⅞" x 3⅞"

Cutting for Remaining Pieces

All measurements include ¼"-wide seam allowances.

Fabrics	Size to Cut
Dark blue	9 strips, 7½" x 42"
Binding fabric	10 strips, 2½" x 42"

Making the Triangle Squares and Blocks

1. Make 504 triangle squares that are half light and half blue and 168 triangle squares that are half blue and half a different blue, following the instructions below for the desired method.

   Method 1: Refer to the instructions on page 6 to make and trim 168 copies of grid 3. If you have cut strips from the fabrics, use the trimmed grids to cut 126 rectangles from the assorted light strips and 210 rectangles from the assorted blue strips. If you are using pieces of fabric, cut them to the same size as the grids if necessary; use the trimmed grids as a guide.

   Pair a blue rectangle with each light rectangle. Pair the remaining blue rectangles together—use two different fabrics for each pair. Make the triangle squares.

   Method 2: Refer to the instructions on page 7 to pair a blue square with each light square. Pair the remaining blue squares together—use two different fabrics for each pair. Make the triangle squares.

Make 504.   Make 168.

2. Arrange the triangle squares as shown to make the Star block. Make 42.

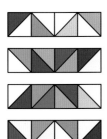
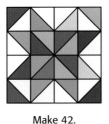

Make 42.

Assembling the Quilt Top

1. Arrange the blocks into seven rows of six blocks each. Stitch the blocks in each row together, and then stitch the rows together.

2. Refer to "Adding Borders" on page 14 to join and trim the dark blue strips to make borders of the correct length. Stitch the top and bottom borders to the quilt top first, and then add the side borders.

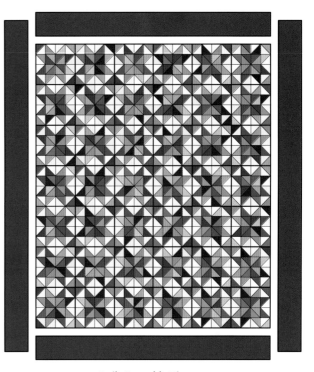

Quilt Assembly Diagram

Finishing

Refer to "Finishing Instructions" on pages 15–18.

1. Layer the quilt top with batting and backing; baste.

2. Quilt as desired.

3. Add a hanging sleeve, if desired.

4. Bind the edges and add a label.

Two-Triangle-Square Tantalizers

Quilts That Combine
Two Triangle-Square Sizes

T is for Turid

Water Lilies

One Step Further I

One Step Further II

Through the Maze

By the Sea

Heart to Heart

T Is for Turid

By Turid Margaret Uren

As my name is Turid, the T block has fascinated me from the first time I saw it. I feel that it is somehow my block, and I just had to make a quilt based on it. I wanted a scrappy, old-fashioned quilt, and I dug into my "not so nice" red scraps to get the right effect. Because this was a project in which I wanted to use what I had and not buy any new fabric, even the sashing strips and borders are made from scraps. —TURID

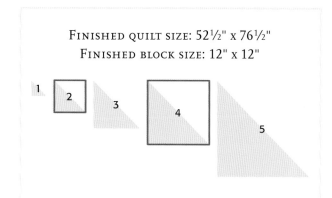

FINISHED QUILT SIZE: 52½" x 76½"
FINISHED BLOCK SIZE: 12" x 12"

OPTIONS: The blocks can be made in three different sizes with a combination of two of the grids given at the back of the book. Finished block sizes are given below for each grid combination.

Grid Combination	Finished Block Size
1 and 2	6" x 6"
2 and 4	12" x 12"
3 and 5	18" x 18"

Materials

Yardage is calculated for the grid 2-and-4 combination using method 1 and is based on 42"-wide fabric. Refer to "Making Changes" on page 8 to recalculate yardage if you use a combination other than grid 2-and-4.

- ▲ 3⅜ yards *total* of assorted reds for blocks and pieced outer border
- ▲ 3⅜ yards *total* of assorted whites and light prints for blocks and pieced outer border
- ▲ ¾ yard *total* of assorted red solids for sashing
- ▲ ½ yard of white for inner border
- ▲ ⅛ yard of yellow solid for sashing squares
- ▲ ⅝ yard of fabric for binding
- ▲ 5 yards of fabric for backing (lengthwise seam)
- ▲ 57" x 81" piece of batting

Cutting for Triangle Squares

All measurements include ¼"-wide seam allowances.

Fabrics	For method 1, cut:	For method 2, cut:
Assorted reds	7 strips, 7" x 42"; or 25 pieces no smaller than 6¼" x 9⅛" for use with grid 2	150 squares, 2⅞" x 2⅞"
	10 strips, 6" x 42"; or 30 pieces no smaller than 5⅜" x 10¼" for use with grid 4	60 squares, 4⅞" x 4⅞"
Assorted whites and light prints	7 strips, 7" x 42"; or 25 pieces no smaller than 6¼" x 9⅛" for use with grid 2	150 squares, 2⅞" x 2⅞"
	10 strips, 6" x 42"; or 30 pieces no smaller than 5⅜" x 10¼" for use with grid 4	60 squares, 4⅞" x 4⅞"

Cutting for Remaining Pieces

All measurements include ¼"-wide seam allowances.

Fabrics	Size to Cut
Assorted red solids	38 strips, 1½" x 12½"
Yellow solid	24 squares, 1½" x 1½"
White for inner border	2 strips, 1½" x 40½"
	4 strips, 2½" x 42"
Binding fabric	7 strips, 2½" x 42"

Making the Triangle Squares and Blocks

1. Make 120 large triangle squares that are half red and half white or light print and 300 small triangle squares that are half red and half white or light print, following the instructions below for the desired method.

    Method 1: Refer to the instructions on page 6 to make and trim 30 copies of grid 4 and 25 copies of grid 2. If you have cut strips from the fabrics, use the trimmed copies of grid 4 to cut 30 rectangles *each* from the assorted red and assorted white or light print 6" x 42" strips. Use the trimmed copies of grid 2 to cut 25 rectangles *each* from the assorted red and assorted white or light print 7" x 42" strips. If you are using individual pieces of fabric, cut them to the same size as the grid indicated in the cutting instructions; use the trimmed grids as a guide.

    Pair each red rectangle with a white or light print rectangle of the same size. Make the triangle squares.

    Method 2: Refer to the instructions on page 7 to pair each red square with a white or light print square of the same size. Make the triangle squares.

Make 120.   Make 300.

2. Stitch one large triangle square and five small triangle squares together as shown. Make 60 units. Set the remaining large triangle squares aside for the outer border.

Make 60.

3. Stitch four units from step 2 together as shown to make the T block. Make 15.

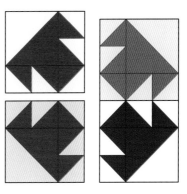

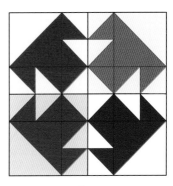

Make 15.

Assembling the Quilt Top

1. To make the block rows, alternately stitch four red solid strips and three T blocks together as shown. Make five rows.

Make 5.

2. To make the sashing rows, stitch four yellow squares and three red solid strips together as shown. Make six rows.

Make 6.

3. Refer to the quilt assembly diagram to alternately stitch the sashing and block rows together, beginning and ending with a sashing row.

4. Refer to "Adding Borders" on page 14 and the quilt assembly diagram to stitch the 1½" x 40½" white strips to the top and bottom edges of the quilt top. Join and trim the 2½" x 42" white strips to make two strips, 2½" x 68½". Stitch the strips to the sides of the quilt top. The quilt top should now measure 44½" x 68½". It is necessary for the quilt top to be exactly this measurement so that the outer pieced border will fit.

5. Stitch 17 of the remaining large triangle squares together as shown to make the outer side borders. Make two. Stitch 13 large triangle squares together as shown to make the outer top and bottom borders. Make two.

Side Borders
Make 2.

Top and Bottom Borders
Make 2.

6. Refer to the quilt assembly diagram to stitch the side borders to the quilt top as shown, and then add the top and bottom borders.

Quilt Assembly Diagram

Finishing

Refer to "Finishing Instructions" on pages 15–18.

1. Layer the quilt top with batting and backing; baste.

2. Quilt as desired.

3. Add a hanging sleeve, if desired.

4. Bind the edges and add a label.

Water Lilies

By Turid Margaret Uren

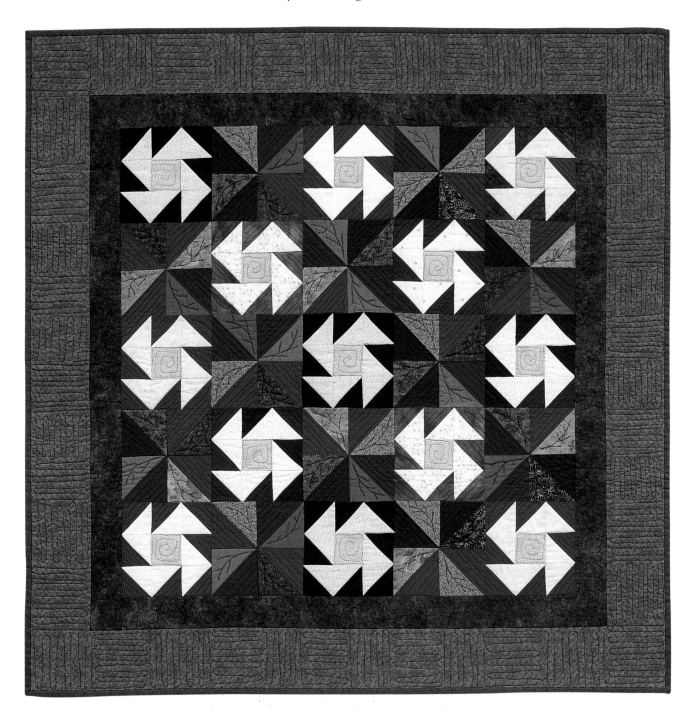

The choice of colors in this quilt made me think of a pond with scattered water lilies. This two-block quilt is quite easy to make. The Water Lily block is a Nine Patch block made with grid 2. The Leaf block is a Four Patch block made with grid 3.—TURID

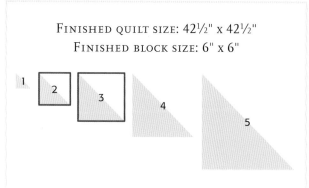

FINISHED QUILT SIZE: 42½" x 42½"
FINISHED BLOCK SIZE: 6" x 6"

OPTIONS: The blocks can be made in two different sizes with a combination of two of the grids given at the back of the book. Finished block sizes are given below for each grid combination.

Grid Combination	Finished Block Size
2 and 3	6" x 6"
4 and 5	12" x 12"

Materials

Yardage is calculated for the grid 2-and-3 combination using method 1 and is based on 42"-wide fabric. Refer to "Making Changes" on page 8 to recalculate yardage if you use a combination other than grid 2-and-3.

- ▲ 1¼ yards *total* of assorted dark blue solids for blocks
- ▲ ¾ yard *total* of assorted whites for blocks
- ▲ ¾ yard of green print for outer border
- ▲ ½ yard *total* of assorted greens for blocks
- ▲ ⅜ yard of blue print for inner border
- ▲ 7" x 15" rectangle *each* of 2 different yellows for blocks
- ▲ ½ yard of fabric for binding
- ▲ 3 yards of fabric for backing
- ▲ 47" x 47" piece of batting

Cutting for Triangle Squares

All measurements include ¼"-wide seam allowances.

Fabrics	For method 1, cut:	For method 2, cut:
Assorted whites	3 strips, 7" x 42"; or 9 pieces no smaller than 6¼" x 9⅛" for use with grid 2	52 squares, 2⅞" x 2⅞"
Assorted dark blue solids	3 strips, 7" x 42"; or 9 pieces no smaller than 6¼" x 9⅛" for use with grid 2	2 squares, 2⅞" x 2⅞"
	3 strips, 5" x 42"; or 12 pieces no smaller than 4⅜" x 8¼" for use with grid 3	24 squares, 3⅞" x 3⅞"
Yellow rectangles	1 rectangle, 6¼" x 9⅛", from *each*	7 squares, 2⅞" x 2⅞", from *each*
	1 square, 3⅜" x 3⅜", from *each*	
Assorted greens	3 strips, 5" x 42"; or 12 pieces no smaller than 4⅜" x 8¼" for use with grid 3	24 squares, 3⅞" x 3⅞"

Cutting for Remaining Pieces

All measurements include ¼"-wide seam allowances.

Fabrics	Size to Cut
Blue print	4 strips, 2½" x 42"
Green print	5 strips, 4½" x 42"
Binding fabric	5 strips, 2½" x 42"

Making the Triangle Squares and Blocks

1. Make the number of each triangle-square combination shown, following the instructions below for the desired method.

    Method 1: Refer to the instructions on page 6 to make and trim 10 copies of grid 2 plus one additional unit, and 12 copies of grid 3. If you have cut strips from the fabrics, use the trimmed copies of grid 2 to cut nine rectangles *each* from the assorted white and assorted dark blue 7" x 42" strips. Use the trimmed copies of grid 3 to cut 12 rectangles *each* from the assorted dark blue and assorted green 5" x 42" strips. If you are using individual pieces of fabric, cut them to the same size as the grid indicated in the cutting instructions; use the trimmed grids as a guide.

    Pair a dark blue grid 2 rectangle with each white rectangle. Pair the yellow rectangles together and the yellow squares together. Pair a dark blue grid 3 rectangle with each green rectangle. Make the triangle squares. Note that the grid method will yield 108 blue-and-white triangle squares but you will only need 104. Also note that this method will yield 14 yellow-and-yellow triangle squares but you will only need 13.

    Method 2: Refer to the instructions on page 7 to pair each white 2⅞" square with a dark blue 2⅞" square. Pair two different yellow squares together. Pair each dark blue 3⅞" square with a green square. Make the triangle squares. Note that you will use 13 yellow-and-yellow triangle squares and have 1 left over.

Make 104.   Make 13.   Make 48.

2. To make the Water Lily blocks, stitch eight white-and-dark-blue triangle squares and one yellow triangle square together as shown. Make 13.

    Note: Identical white-and-dark-blue triangle squares were used in each block in the featured quilt. This is easier to plan for if you use individual rectangles, but it can also be accomplished by cutting a few more rectangles from strips. However, you will have more leftover triangle squares. Two pairs of rectangles will yield exactly the amount needed for three blocks.

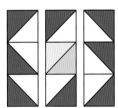 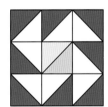

Make 13.

3. To make the Leaf blocks, stitch four green-and-dark-blue triangle squares together as shown. Make 12.

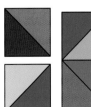 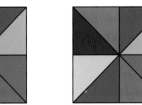

Make 12.

Assembling the Quilt Top

1. Refer to the quilt assembly diagram to arrange the Water Lily and Leaf blocks into five horizontal rows as shown. Stitch the blocks in each row together, and then stitch the rows together.

2. Refer to "Adding Borders" on page 14 and the quilt assembly diagram to trim the blue print strips as needed to make inner borders of the correct length. Stitch the inner top and bottom borders to the quilt top first, and then add the inner side borders. Join and trim the green print strips as needed to make outer-border strips of the correct length. Stitch the outer top and bottom borders to the quilt top first, and then add the outer side borders.

Quilt Assembly Diagram

Finishing

Refer to "Finishing Instructions" on pages 15–18.

1. Layer the quilt top with batting and backing; baste.

2. Quilt as desired.

3. Add a hanging sleeve, if desired.

4. Bind the edges and add a label.

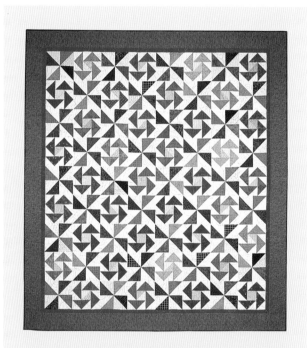

"Field of Flowers"
by Turid Margaret Uren, 89" x 98".
Machine quilted by AKD Quilteteknikk.

By choosing a light fabric for the background and bright scraps for the flowers, you'll achieve a very different look from "Water Lilies," almost like a field of summer flowers. The blocks in this quilt finish to 9" square. Grid 3 was used to make the Flower blocks; the Leaf blocks were made from a grid of 5 ⅜" squares, which is not available in this book.

One Step Further I

By Turid Margaret Uren

This quilt and "One Step Further II" on page 49 were the result of my experiment to see what would happen if I used the same block layout but changed the colors. It really brought me "one step further" and gave me inspiration to continue the journey.—TURID

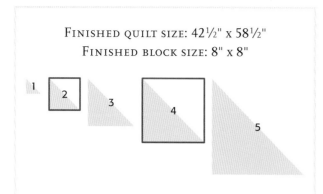

FINISHED QUILT SIZE: 42½" x 58½"
FINISHED BLOCK SIZE: 8" x 8"

OPTIONS: The blocks in this quilt can be made in three different sizes with a combination of two of the grids given at the back of the book. Finished block sizes are given below for each grid combination.

Grid Combination	Finished Block Size
1 and 2	4" x 4"
2 and 4	8" x 8"
3 and 5	12" x 12"

Materials

Yardage is calculated for the grid 2-and-4 combination using method 1 and is based on 42"-wide fabric. Refer to "Making Changes" on page 8 to recalculate yardage if you use a combination other than grid 2-and-4.

▲ 1⅞ yards *total* of assorted blacks for blocks and pieced inner border
▲ 1⅝ yards *total* of assorted whites for blocks and pieced inner border
▲ ¾ yard of black solid for outer border
▲ ½ yard *total* of assorted reds for blocks
▲ ⅜ yard of red solid for middle border
▲ ⅝ yard of fabric for binding
▲ 3 yards of fabric for backing (crosswise seam)
▲ 47" x 63" piece of batting

Cutting for Triangle Squares

All measurements include ¼"-wide seam allowances.

Fabrics	For method 1, cut:	For method 2, cut:
Assorted blacks	3 strips, 7" x 42"; or 11 pieces no smaller than 6¼" x 9⅛" for use with grid 2	64 squares, 2⅞" x 2⅞"
	6 strips, 6" x 42"; or 16 pieces no smaller than 5⅜" x 10¼" for use with grid 4	32 squares, 4⅞" x 4⅞"
Assorted whites	3 strips, 7" x 42"; or 11 pieces no smaller than 6¼" x 9⅛" for use with grid 2	64 squares, 2⅞" x 2⅞"
	4 strips, 6" x 42"; or 10 pieces no smaller than 5⅜" x 10¼" for use with grid 4	20 squares, 4⅞" x 4⅞"
Assorted reds	2 strips, 6" x 42"; or 6 pieces no smaller than 5⅜" x 10¼" for use with grid 4	12 squares, 4⅞" x 4⅞"

Cutting for Remaining Pieces

All measurements include ¼"-wide seam allowances.

Fabrics	Size to Cut
Red solid	5 strips, 1½" x 42"
Black solid	5 strips, 4½" x 42"
Binding fabric	6 strips, 2½" x 42"

Making the Triangle Squares and Blocks

1. Make the number of each triangle-square combination shown, following the instructions below for the desired method.

   Method 1: Refer to the instructions on page 6 to make and trim 11 copies of grid 2 and 16 copies of grid 4. If you have cut strips from the fabrics, use the trimmed copies of grid 2 to cut 11 rectangles *each* from the assorted black and assorted white 7" x 42" strips. Use the trimmed copies of grid 4 to cut 16 rectangles from the assorted black 6" x 42" strips, 10 rectangles from the assorted white 6" x 42" strips, and 6 rectangles from the assorted red 6" x 42" strips. If you are using individual pieces of fabric, cut them to the same size as the grid indicated in the cutting instructions; use the trimmed grids as a guide.

   Pair a black grid 2 rectangle with each white grid 2 rectangle. Pair a black grid 4 rectangle with each white and red grid 4 rectangle. Make the triangle squares. Note that the grid method will yield 132 black-and-white triangle squares and you will use 128.

   Method 2: Refer to the instructions on page 7 to pair each black square with a white or red square of the same size. Make the triangle squares.

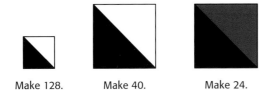

   Make 128.   Make 40.   Make 24.

2. Stitch four grid 2 triangle squares together as shown. Make 32 units.

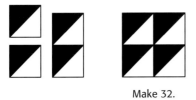

   Make 32.

3. Stitch four units from step 2 together as shown to make blocks A and B, being careful to rotate the triangle squares in the correct direction for each block. Make six of block A and two of block B.

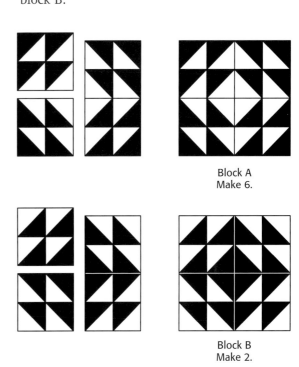

   Block A
   Make 6.

   Block B
   Make 2.

4. Stitch four grid 4 triangle squares together as shown to make block C. Make seven. Set the remaining grid 4 triangle squares aside for the pieced inner border.

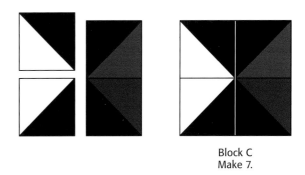

   Block C
   Make 7.

Assembling the Quilt Top

1. Refer to the quilt assembly diagram on page 48 to arrange blocks A, B, and C into five horizontal rows of three blocks each as shown. Stitch the blocks in each row together, and then stitch the rows together.

2. Stitch the remaining grid 4 triangle squares together as shown to make the pieced inner-border strips.

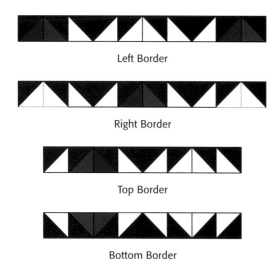

Left Border

Right Border

Top Border

Bottom Border

3. Stitch the pieced inner side borders to the quilt top as shown, and then add the inner top and bottom borders.

4. Refer to "Adding Borders" on page 14 to join and trim the red solid strips as needed to make middle borders of the correct length. Stitch the middle top and bottom borders to the quilt top first, and then add the middle side borders. Repeat with the black solid outer-border strips.

Quilt Assembly Diagram

Finishing

Refer to "Finishing Instructions" on pages 15–18.

1. Layer the quilt top with batting and backing; baste.

2. Quilt as desired.

3. Add a hanging sleeve, if desired.

4. Bind the edges and add a label.

One Step Further II

By Turid Margaret Uren

*The three-dimensional effect in this variation is interesting! And it was
accomplished by using all white-and-black triangle squares
and rotating their placement in the blocks.*—TURID

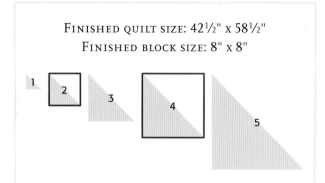

FINISHED QUILT SIZE: 42½" x 58½"
FINISHED BLOCK SIZE: 8" x 8"

OPTIONS: The blocks in this quilt can be made in three different sizes with a combination of two of the grids given at the back of the book. Finished block sizes are given below for each grid combination.

Grid Combination	Finished Block Size
1 and 2	4" x 4"
2 and 4	8" x 8"
3 and 5	12" x 12"

Materials

Yardage is calculated for the grid 2-and-4 combination using method 1 and is based on 42"-wide fabric. Refer to "Making Changes" on page 8 to recalculate yardage if you use a combination other than grid 2-and-4.

- ▲ 1⅞ yards of assorted blacks
- ▲ 1⅞ yards of assorted whites
- ▲ ¾ yard of black solid for outer border
- ▲ ⅜ yard of red solid for inner border
- ▲ ⅝ yard of fabric for binding
- ▲ 3 yards of fabric for backing (crosswise seam)
- ▲ 47" x 63" piece of batting

Cutting for Triangle Squares

All measurements include ¼"-wide seam allowances.

Fabrics	For method 1, cut:	For method 2, cut:
Assorted blacks	3 strips, 7" x 42"; or 11 pieces no smaller than 6¼" x 9⅛" for use with grid 2	64 squares, 2⅞" x 2⅞"
	6 strips, 6" x 42"; or 16 pieces no smaller than 5⅜" x 10¼" for use with grid 4	32 squares, 4⅞" x 4⅞"
Assorted whites	3 strips, 7" x 42"; or 11 pieces no smaller than 6¼" x 9⅛" for use with grid 2	64 squares, 2⅞" x 2⅞"
	6 strips, 6" x 42"; or 16 pieces no smaller than 5⅜" x 10¼" for use with grid 4	32 squares, 4⅞" x 4⅞"

Cutting for Remaining Pieces

All measurements include ¼"-wide seam allowances.

Fabrics	Size to Cut
Red solid	5 strips, 1½" x 42"
Black solid	5 strips, 4½" x 42"
Binding fabric	6 strips, 2½" x 42"

Making the Triangle Squares and Blocks

1. Make 128 small black-and-white triangle squares and 64 large black-and-white triangle squares, following the instructions below for the desired method.

   Method 1: Refer to the instructions on page 6 to make and trim 11 copies of grid 2 and 16 copies of grid 4. If you have cut the strips from the fabrics, use the trimmed copies of grid 2 to cut 11 rectangles *each* from the assorted black and assorted white 7" x 42" strips. Use the trimmed copies of grid 4 to cut 16 rectangles *each* from the assorted black and assorted white 6" x 42" strips. If you are using individual pieces of fabric, cut them to the same size as the grid indicated in the cutting instructions; use the trimmed grids as a guide.

   Pair each black rectangle with a white rectangle of the same size. Make the triangle squares. Note that the grid method will yield 132 grid 2 triangle squares and you will use 128.

   Method 2: Refer to the instructions on page 7 to pair each black square with a white square of the same size. Make the triangle squares.

Make 128.

Make 64.

2. Stitch four grid 2 triangle squares together as shown. Make 32 units.

Make 32.

3. Stitch four units from step 2 together as shown to make block A, being careful to rotate the triangle squares in the correct direction to create the pattern. Make eight.

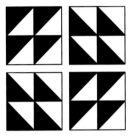
Block A
Make 8.

4. Stitch four grid 4 triangle squares together as shown to make block B. Make seven. Set the remaining grid 4 triangle squares aside for the pieced inner border.

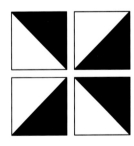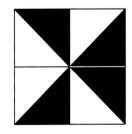
Block B
Make 7.

Assembling the Quilt Top

1. Refer to the quilt assembly diagram on page 52 to arrange blocks A and B into five horizontal rows of three blocks each as shown. Stitch the blocks in each row together, and then stitch the rows together.

2. Stitch the remaining grid 4 triangle squares together as shown to make the pieced inner-border strips.

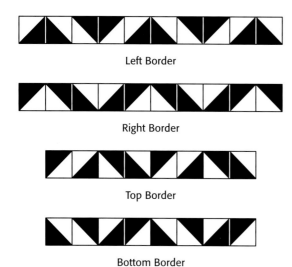

Left Border

Right Border

Top Border

Bottom Border

3. Stitch the pieced inner side borders to the quilt top as shown, and then add the inner top and bottom borders.

4. Refer to "Adding Borders" on page 14 to join and trim the red solid strips as needed to make middle borders of the correct length. Stitch the middle top and bottom borders to the quilt top first, and then add the middle side borders. Repeat with the black solid outer-border strips.

Quilt Assembly Diagram

Finishing

Refer to "Finishing Instructions" on pages 15–18.

1. Layer the quilt top with batting and backing; baste.

2. Quilt as desired.

3. Add a hanging sleeve, if desired.

4. Bind the edges and add a label.

Through the Maze

By Turid Margaret Uren

While playing with the blocks from "One Step Further I," I decided to see what would happen if I changed the layout to a diagonal setting, simplified the blocks, and used only two colors. By doing so, I created a maze of sorts. To find a way out of the quilt, follow the borders. To get the right effect and at the same time put some excitement into the quilt, your choice of fabrics is important. Be bold, but stay away from busy prints!—TURID

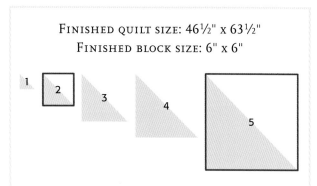

FINISHED QUILT SIZE: 46½" x 63½"
FINISHED BLOCK SIZE: 6" x 6"

OPTIONS: The blocks can be made in two different sizes with a combination of two of the grids given at the back of the book. Finished block sizes are given below for each grid combination.

Grid Combination	Finished Block Size
1 and 3	3" x 3"
2 and 5	6" x 6"

Materials

Yardage is calculated for the grid 2-and-5 combination using method 1 and is based on 42"-wide fabric. Refer to "Making Changes" on page 8 to recalculate yardage if you use a combination other than grid 2-and-5.

- ▲ 2¼ yards *total* of assorted blacks for blocks
- ▲ 2¼ yards *total* of assorted reds for blocks
- ▲ 1⅛ yards of black solid for borders and binding
- ▲ 1⅛ yards of red solid for borders and binding
- ▲ 3⅛ yards of fabric for backing (crosswise seam)
- ▲ 51" x 68" piece of batting

Cutting for Triangle Squares

All measurements include ¼"-wide seam allowances.

Fabrics	For method 1, cut:	For method 2, cut:
Assorted blacks	5 strips, 7" x 42"; or 18 pieces no smaller than 6¼" x 9⅛" for use with grid 2	108 squares, 2⅞" x 2⅞"
	2 strips, 8" x 42"; or 8 pieces no smaller than 7⅜" x 7⅜" for use with grid 5	8 squares, 6⅞" x 6⅞"
Assorted reds	5 strips, 7" x 42"; or 18 pieces no smaller than 6¼" x 9⅛" for use with grid 2	108 squares, 2⅞" x 2⅞"
	2 strips, 8" x 42"; or 8 pieces no smaller than 7⅜" x 7⅜" for use with grid 5	8 squares, 6⅞" x 6⅞"

Cutting for Remaining Pieces

All measurements include ¼"-wide seam allowances.

Fabrics	Size to Cut
Red solid	6 strips, 2½" x 42"
	4 strips, 4½" x 42"
Black solid	6 strips, 2½" x 42"
	4 strips, 4½" x 42"

Continued on page 55

Continued from page 54

Remaining assorted reds or red solid	3 squares, 6⅞" x 6⅞"; cut each square in half once diagonally to yield 6 side setting triangles. You will use 5 and have 1 left over.
	2 squares, 7¼" x 7¼"
	1 square, 5½" x 5½"; cut the square in half once diagonally to yield 2 corner setting triangles
Remaining assorted blacks or black solid	3 squares, 6⅞" x 6⅞"; cut each square in half once diagonally to yield 6 side setting triangles. You will use 5 and have 1 left over.
	2 squares, 7¼" x 7¼"
	1 square, 5½" x 5½"; cut the square in half once diagonally to yield 2 corner setting triangles

Making the Triangle Squares and Blocks

1. Make 216 small triangle squares that are half red and half black and 15 large triangle squares that are half red and half black, following the instructions below for the desired method.

    Method 1: Refer to the instructions on page 6 to make and trim 18 copies of grid 2 and 8 copies of grid 5. If you have cut strips from the fabrics, use the trimmed copies of grid 2 to cut 18 rectangles *each* from the assorted red and assorted black 7" x 42" strips. Use the trimmed copies of grid 5 to cut 8 squares *each* from the assorted red and assorted black 8" x 42" strips. If you are using individual pieces of fabric, cut them to the same size as the grid indicated in the cutting instructions; use the trimmed grids as a guide.

    Pair each red rectangle with a black rectangle. Pair each red square with a black square. Make the triangle squares. Note that the grid method will yield 16 large triangle squares and you will use 15.

    Method 2: Refer to the instructions on page 7 to pair each red square with a black square of the same size. Make the triangle squares. Note

    that you will use 15 large triangle squares and have one left over.

    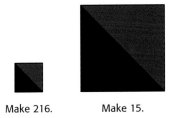

    Make 216.   Make 15.

2. Stitch nine small triangle squares together as shown to make the Maze block. Make 24.

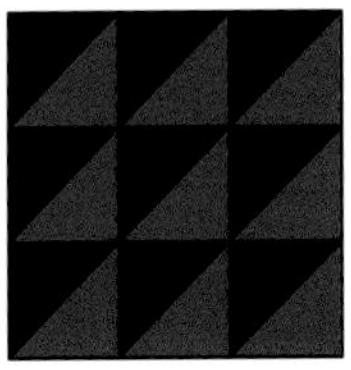

    Make 24.

3. Refer to method 2 on page 7 to make four triangle squares from the black and red 7¼" squares. Cut three of the triangle squares in half diagonally. These are the half-blocks that will be used as the top and bottom setting triangles. Discard the remaining triangle square or set it aside to use in another project.

Assembling the Quilt Top

1. Stitch the Maze blocks, the large triangle squares, and the setting triangles into nine diagonal rows as shown. Stitch the pieces in each row together, and then stitch the rows together. Add the corner setting triangles last.

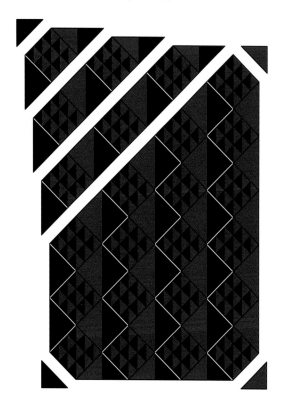

2. Refer to "Adding Borders" on page 14 and the quilt assembly diagram to trim one red and one black 2½" x 42" strip *each* to the correct length for the top and bottom borders. Stitch the strips to the top and bottom edges of the quilt top, being careful of color placement. Join and trim two of the remaining red 2½" x 42" strips to make a side border of the correct length; repeat with two of the remaining black 2½" x 42" strips. Stitch the strips to the sides of the quilt top, again being careful of color placement.

3. Join and trim the red and black 4½" x 42" strips to make outer borders of the correct length. Stitch the top and bottom borders to the quilt top first, and then add the side borders, being careful of color placement.

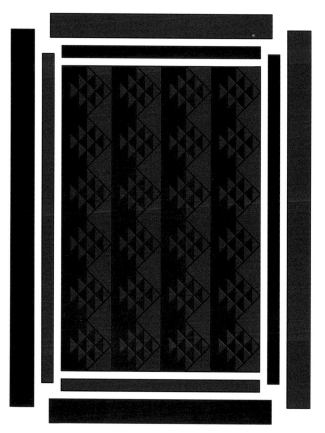

Quilt Assembly Diagram

Finishing

Refer to "Finishing Instructions" on pages 15–18.

1. Layer the quilt top with batting and backing; baste.

2. Quilt as desired.

3. Add a hanging sleeve, if desired.

4. Bind the edges of the quilt top so that the red borders are bound with the red fabric and the black borders are bound with the black fabric. Add a label.

By the Sea

By Kristin Bergljot Johannessen. Machine quilted by AKD Quilteteknikk.

I live by the sea, and when I look out of my windows I see an ever-changing picture of blue and aqua, which always gives me great pleasure. These colors also happen to be among my favorites and are used throughout my house. Since I am a crew member on my son's sailing boat, I wanted a maritime theme for the quilting on this project. I was very pleased to find out, when the quilt came back from the machine quilter, that she had used sailboats and waves in the outer border. —KRISTIN

FINISHED QUILT SIZE: 58½" x 78½"
FINISHED LARGE BLOCK SIZE: 6" x 6"
FINISHED SMALL BLOCK SIZE: 4" x 4"

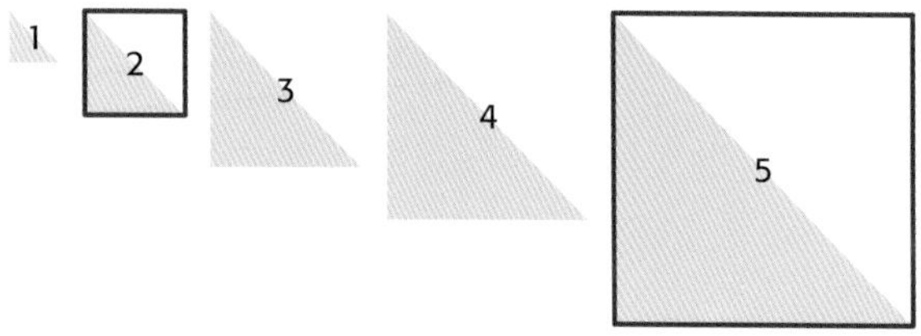

1 2 3 4 5

OPTIONS: The blocks in this quilt can be made with a combination of two of the grids given at the back of the book. Finished block sizes are given below for each grid combination.

Grid Combination	Finished Large Block	Finished Small Block (Sashing)
1 and 3	3" x 3"	2" x 2"
2 and 5	6" x 6"	4" x 4"

Materials

Yardage is calculated for the grid 2-and-5 combination using method 1 and is based on 42"-wide fabric. Refer to "Making Changes" on page 8 to recalculate yardage if you use a combination other than grid 2-and-5.

▲ 3¼ yards *total* of assorted tans for blocks and sashing
▲ 3¼ yards *total* of assorted blues, greens, and aquas for blocks and sashing
▲ 1¼ yards of dark blue for outer border
▲ ⅝ yard of aqua for inner border
▲ ⅝ yard of fabric for binding
▲ 4¾ yards of fabric for backing (lengthwise seam)
▲ 62" x 82" piece of batting

Cutting for Triangle Squares

All measurements include ¼"-wide seam allowances.

Fabrics	For method 1, cut:	For method 2, cut:
Assorted tans	11 strips, 7" x 42"; or 41 pieces no smaller than 6¼" x 9⅛" for use with grid 2	244 squares, 2⅞" x 2⅞"
	3 strips, 8" x 42"; or 12 pieces no smaller than 7⅜" x 7⅜" for use with grid 5	12 squares, 6⅞" x 6⅞"
Assorted blues, greens, and aquas	11 strips, 7" x 42"; or 41 pieces no smaller than 6¼" x 9⅛" for use with grid 2	244 squares, 2⅞" x 2⅞"
	3 strips, 8" x 42"; or 12 pieces no smaller than 7⅜" x 7⅜" for use with grid 5	12 squares, 6⅞" x 6⅞"

Cutting for Remaining Pieces

All measurements include ¼"-wide seam allowances.

Fabrics	Size to Cut
Aqua for inner border	7 strips, 2" x 42"
Dark blue	7 strips, 5½" x 42"
Binding fabric	7 strips, 2½" x 42"

Making the Triangle Squares and Pieced Sashing

1. Make 488 small triangle squares and 24 large triangle squares that are half tan and half blue, green, or aqua, following the instructions below for the desired method.

   Method 1: Refer to the instructions on page 6 to make and trim 41 copies of grid 2 and 12 copies of grid 5. If you have cut strips from the fabrics, use the trimmed copies of grid 2 to cut 41 rectangles *each* from the assorted tan and assorted blue, green, and aqua 7" x 42" strips. Use the trimmed copies of grid 5 to cut 12 squares *each* from the assorted tan and assorted blue, green, and aqua 8" x 42" strips. If you are using individual pieces of fabric, cut them to the same size as the grid indicated in the cutting instructions; use the trimmed grids as a guide.

   Pair each tan rectangle with a blue, green, or aqua rectangle. Make the triangle squares. Note that the grid method will yield 492 triangle squares and you will use 488. Repeat with the tan and blue, green, and aqua squares.

   Method 2: Refer to the instructions on page 7 to pair each tan square with a blue, green, or aqua square of the same size. Make the triangle squares.

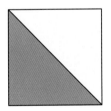

Make 488.   Make 24.

2. Stitch six small triangle squares together as shown to make the sashing strips. Make 58.

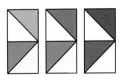
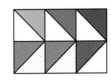

Make 58.

3. Stitch four small triangle squares together as shown to make sashing blocks A and B. Make 17 of block A and 18 of block B.

Sashing Block A   Sashing Block B
Make 17.   Make 18.

Assembling the Quilt Top

1. To make the block rows, stitch five sashing strips and four large triangle squares together as shown. Be careful to orient the pieces in the correct direction. Make six rows.

Make 6.

2. To make the sashing rows, arrange the sashing blocks and sashing strips to make rows 1 and 2. Be careful to orient the strips in the correct direction and arrange the blocks in alternate positions. Make four of row 1 and three of row 2.

Row 1
Make 4.

Row 2
Make 3.

3. Stitch the sashing and block rows together as shown. Be careful to rotate the block rows so that the dark half of each triangle square is in the correct position.

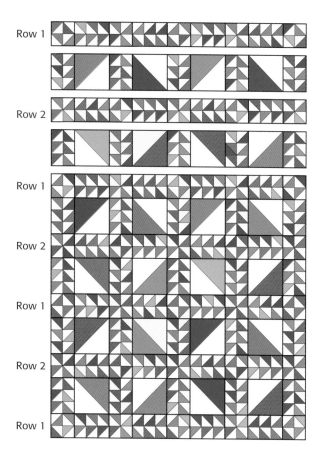

4. Refer to "Adding Borders" on page 14 to join and trim the aqua strips to make inner borders of the correct length. Refer to the quilt assembly diagram to stitch the top and bottom borders to the quilt top first, and then add the side borders. Repeat for the dark blue outer-border strips.

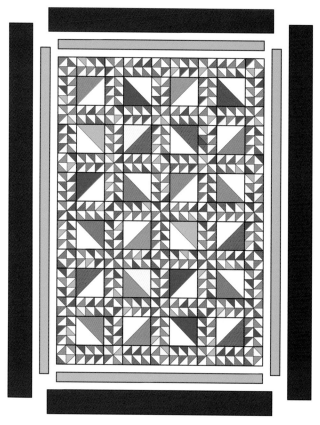

Quilt Assembly Diagram

Finishing

Refer to "Finishing Instructions" on pages 15–18.

1. Layer the quilt top with batting and backing; baste.

2. Quilt as desired.

3. Add a hanging sleeve, if desired.

4. Bind the edges and add a label.

Heart to Heart

By Turid Margaret Uren. Machine quilted by AKD Quilteteknikk.

To give a quilt with hearts on it is a statement of love. A heart quilt is a symbol of love, warmth, and caring, and at the same time it is there for you to wrap around you any time you need some extra comfort. Once again my scraps gave me the inspiration for a project. Placing the red hearts on a black background brings out the warmth in the hearts, and the red inner border keeps the hearts in place. The grid combination given here is the only option available with the grids at the back of the book.—TURID

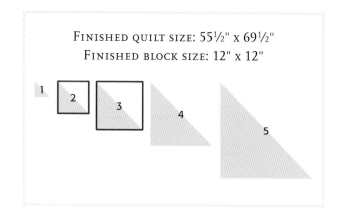

FINISHED QUILT SIZE: 55½" x 69½"
FINISHED BLOCK SIZE: 12" x 12"

Materials

Yardage is calculated for the grid 2-and-3 combination using method 1 and is based on 42"-wide fabric.

▲ 2⅜ yards *total* of assorted blacks for blocks

▲ 2 yards *total* of assorted reds for blocks

▲ 1½ yards of black solid or small print for inner and outer borders

▲ ⅝ yard of black solid for sashing

▲ ½ yard of red solid for middle border

▲ ⅝ yard of fabric for binding

▲ 3⅝ yards of fabric for backing (crosswise seam)

▲ 60" x 74" piece of batting

Cutting for Triangle Squares

All measurements include ¼"-wide seam allowances.

Fabrics	For method 1, cut:	For method 2, cut:
Assorted blacks	7 strips, 7" x 42"; or 26 pieces no smaller than 6¼" x 9⅛" for use with grid 2	156 squares, 2⅞" x 2⅞"
	5 strips, 5" x 42"; or 18 pieces no smaller than 4⅜" x 8¼" for use with grid 3	36 squares, 3⅞" x 3⅞"
Assorted reds	3 strips, 7" x 42"; or 10 pieces no smaller than 6¼" x 9⅛" for use with grid 2	60 squares, 2⅞" x 2⅞"
	8 strips, 5" x 42"; or 30 pieces no smaller than 4⅜" x 8¼" for use with grid 3	60 squares, 3⅞" x 3⅞"

Cutting for Remaining Pieces

All measurements include ¼"-wide seam allowances.

Fabrics	Size to Cut
Black solid for sashing	6 strips, 2½" x 42"; crosscut the strips into:
	8 strips, 2½" x 12½"
	3 strips, 2½" x 40½"
Black for inner and outer borders	5 strips, 2½" x 42"
	6 strips, 4½" x 42"
Red solid	6 strips, 2" x 42"
Binding fabric	7 strips, 2½" x 42"

Making the Triangle Squares and Blocks

1. Make the number of each large and small triangle-square combination shown, following the instructions below for the desired method.

   Method 1: Refer to the instructions on page 6 to make and trim 18 copies of grid 2 and 24 copies of grid 3. If you have cut strips from the fabrics, use the trimmed copies of grid 2 to cut 26 rectangles from the assorted black 7" x 42" strips and 10 rectangles from the assorted red 7" x 42" strips. Use the trimmed copies of grid 3 to cut 18 rectangles from the assorted black 5" x 42" strips and 30 rectangles from the assorted red 5" x 42" strips. If you are using individual pieces of fabric, cut them to the same size as the grid indicated in the cutting instructions; use the trimmed grids as a guide.

   Using the grid 2 rectangles, pair 11 black rectangles with a different black rectangle. Pair each of the remaining black rectangles with a red rectangle. Pair the remaining red rectangles together. Make the small triangle squares.

   Using the grid 3 rectangles, pair 3 black rectangles with a different black rectangle. Pair each of the remaining black rectangles with a red rectangle. Pair the remaining red rectangles together. Make the large triangle squares.

   Method 2: Refer to the instructions on page 7 to make the small and large triangle squares. Using the 2⅞" squares, make the small triangle squares by pairing 66 black squares with a different black square. Pair each of the remaining black squares with a red square. Pair the remaining red squares together. Make the small triangle squares.

   Using the 3⅞" squares, make the large triangle squares by pairing 6 black squares with a different black square. Pair each of the remaining black squares with a red square. Pair the remaining red squares together. Make the large triangle squares.

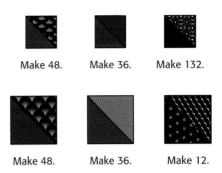

Make 48.   Make 36.   Make 132.

Make 48.   Make 36.   Make 12.

2. Stitch the large triangle squares together as shown. Make six Large Heart blocks.

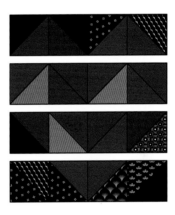

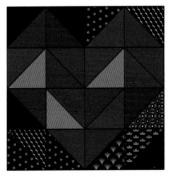

Make 6.

3. Stitch the small triangle squares together as shown. Make six Small Heart blocks.

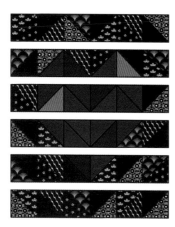

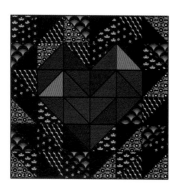

Make 6.

Assembling the Quilt Top

1. Stitch the blocks and 2½" x 12½" black sashing strips together to make block rows 1 and 2 as shown. Make two of each row.

Row 1
Make 2.

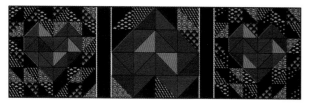

Row 2
Make 2.

2. Refer to the quilt assembly diagram to stitch the block rows and 2½" x 40½" black sashing strips together as shown.

3. Refer to "Adding Borders" on page 14 and the quilt assembly diagram to join and trim the 2½" x 42" black border strips to make inner borders of the correct length. Stitch the top and bottom border strips to the quilt top first, and then add the side borders. Repeat to add the red middle-border strips and the 4½"-wide black outer-border strips.

Quilt Assembly Diagram

Finishing

Refer to "Finishing Instructions" on pages 15–18.

1. Layer the quilt top with batting and backing; baste.

2. Quilt as desired.

3. Add a hanging sleeve, if desired.

4. Bind the edges and add a label.

Combination Creations

Projects That Incorporate Other Shapes into the Mix

Windmills

Down the Road

Transforming Maple Leaves

Tea Time

Monkey Wrench?

One of My Favorites

Starry Night

Windmills

By Turid Margaret Uren

*Arranged just right, groups of four triangle squares become windmills that twist and turn across
this fun quilt. Plain squares between the Windmill blocks allow them room to twirl,
while an easy sawtooth border, also made from triangle squares, provides the frame.*—TURID

FINISHED QUILT SIZE: 42½" x 42½"
FINISHED BLOCK SIZE: 6" x 6"

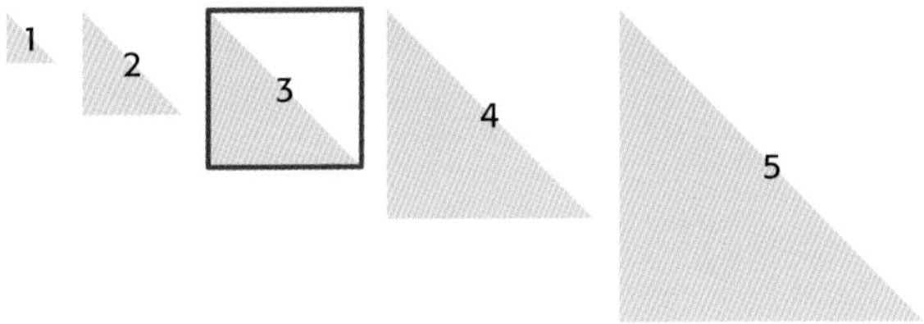

1 2 3 4 5

OPTIONS: The blocks can be made in five different sizes with any of the grids given at the back of the book. Finished block sizes are given below for each grid size.

Grid	Finished Block Size
1	2" x 2"
2	4" x 4"
3	6" x 6"
4	8" x 8"
5	12" x 12"

Materials

Yardage is calculated for grid 3 using method 1 and is based on 42"-wide fabric. Refer to "Making Changes" on page 8 to recalculate yardage if you use a grid size other than grid 3.

▲ 1½ yards *total* of assorted whites for triangle squares and plain squares
▲ ¾ yard *total* of assorted pinks for blocks
▲ ¾ yard *total* of assorted light blues for blocks
▲ ½ yard of white for inner border
▲ ½ yard of light blue solid for binding
▲ 3 yards of fabric for backing
▲ 46" x 46" piece of batting

Cutting for Triangle Squares

All measurements include ¼"-wide seam allowances.

Fabrics	For method 1, cut:	For method 2, cut:
Assorted whites	7 strips, 5" x 42"; or 27 pieces no smaller than 4⅜" x 8¼"	52 squares, 3⅞" x 3⅞"
Assorted pinks	4 strips, 5" x 42"; or 14 pieces no smaller than 4⅜" x 8¼"	27 squares, 3⅞" x 3⅞"
Assorted light blues	4 strips, 5" x 42"; or 13 pieces no smaller than 4⅜" x 8¼"	25 squares, 3⅞" x 3⅞"

Cutting for Remaining Pieces

All measurements include ¼"-wide seam allowances.

Fabrics	Size to Cut
Assorted whites	12 squares, 6½" x 6½"
White for inner border	2 strips, 3½" x 30½"
	2 strips, 3½" x 36½"
Binding fabric	5 strips, 2½" x 42"

Making the
Triangle Squares and Blocks

1. Make 54 triangle squares that are half white and half pink and 50 triangle squares that are half white and half light blue, following the instructions below for the desired method.

   Method 1: Refer to the instructions on page 6 to make and trim 27 copies of grid 3. If you have cut strips from the fabrics, use the trimmed grids to cut 27 assorted white rectangles, 14 assorted pink rectangles, and 13 assorted blue rectangles. If you are using pieces of fabric, cut them to the same size as the trimmed grids if necessary; use the grids as a guide.

   Pair an assorted white rectangle with each assorted blue and assorted pink rectangle. Make the triangle squares. You will have two extra pink-and-white triangle squares and six extra blue-and-white triangle squares. Discard them or set them aside to use in another project.

   Method 2: Refer to the instructions on page 7 to pair an assorted white 3⅞" square with each assorted blue and assorted pink 3⅞" square. Make the triangle squares.

Make 50.   Make 54.

2. Join four identical blue-and-white triangle squares as shown. Repeat to make a total of six blue-and-white Windmill blocks. Join four identical pink-and-white triangle squares as shown. Repeat to make a total of seven pink-and-white Windmill blocks. Set aside the remaining triangle squares for the outer border.

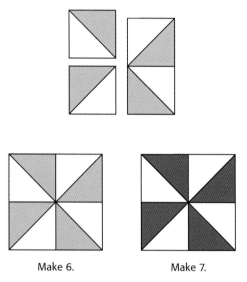

Make 6.   Make 7.

Assembling the Quilt Top

1. Arrange the Windmill blocks and white 6½" squares into five rows as shown. Stitch the blocks and squares in each row together, and then stitch the rows together.

2. Refer to the quilt assembly diagram to stitch the white 3½" x 30½" strips to the top and bottom edges of the quilt top. Stitch the white 3½" x 36½" strips to the sides of the quilt top. It is necessary for the top to measure 36½" x 36½" at this point so that the pieced outer-border strips will fit.

Note: If you have chosen to make your quilt using another size triangle square, the inner border must be cut the same width as the triangle square used *with seam allowances included*. For example, if you used grid 2 triangle squares, you need to cut your border strips 2½" wide.

3. Arrange the remaining triangle squares as shown to make the outer-border strips.

Top and Bottom Borders
Make 2.

Side Borders
Make 2.

4. Stitch the top and bottom borders to the quilt top first, and then add the side borders.

Quilt Assembly Diagram

Finishing

Refer to "Finishing Instructions" on pages 15–18.

1. Layer the quilt top with batting and backing; baste.

2. Quilt as desired.

3. Add a hanging sleeve, if desired.

4. Bind the edges and add a label.

"Baby Windmills"
by Turid Margaret Uren, 24" x 24".

This variation was made using grid 2 triangle squares and no solid squares between the blocks.

Down the Road

By Turid Margaret Uren

*On my experimental journey with "One Step Further I" (page 45) and "Through the Maze" (page 53), I went "down the road" a bit more with the design, adding more colors, making some changes to the blocks, and adding an alternate block that is a plain square and measures the same as the pieced block. Once again something exciting emerged. This diagonal effect is in fact set in a straight layout. It works best with solid-color fabrics or fabrics with a small print. Make sure that there is a good contrast between colors in the triangle squares.—*TURID

FINISHED QUILT SIZE: 61½" x 73½"
FINISHED BLOCK SIZE: 6" x 6"

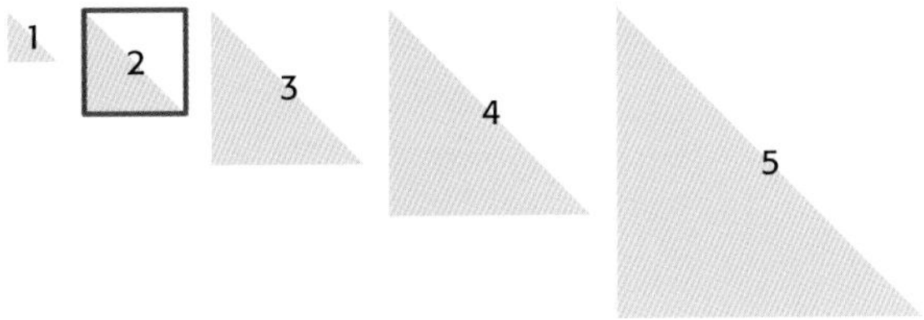

Materials

Yardage is calculated for grid 2 using method 1 and is based on 42"-wide fabric. Refer to "Making Changes" on page 8 to recalculate yardage if you use a grid size other than grid 2.

- ▲ 1⅜ yards *each* of red, dark blue, and yellow solid or small print for blocks
- ▲ 1⅜ yards of red for outer border
- ▲ ¾ yard of aqua #1 solid or small print for blocks
- ▲ ½ yard of aqua #2 solid or small print for blocks
- ▲ ⅜ yard of dark blue for inner border
- ▲ ⅝ yard of fabric for binding
- ▲ 4⅛ yards of fabric for backing (lengthwise seam)
- ▲ 66" x 78" piece of batting

OPTIONS: The blocks can be made in five different sizes with the grids given at the back of the book. Finished block sizes are given below for each grid size.

Grid	Finished Block Size
1	3" x 3"
2	6" x 6"
3	9" x 9"
4	12" x 12"
5	18" x 18"

Cutting for Triangle Squares

All measurements include ¼"-wide seam allowances.

Fabrics	For method 1, cut:	For method 2, cut:
Red, dark blue, and yellow solid or small print	4 strips, 7" x 42", of *each* color; or 16 pieces no smaller than 6¼" x 9⅛", of *each* color	90 squares, 2⅞" x 2⅞", of *each* color
Aqua #1	3 strips, 7" x 42"; or 11 pieces no smaller than 6¼" x 9⅛"	63 squares, 2⅞" x 2⅞"
Aqua #2	2 strips, 7" x 42"; or 5 pieces no smaller than 6¼" x 9⅛"	27 squares, 2⅞" x 2⅞"

Cutting for Remaining Pieces

All measurements include ¼"-wide seam allowances.

Fabrics	Size to Cut
Red, dark blue, and yellow solid or small print	10 squares, 6½" x 6½", of *each* color
Aqua #1	7 squares, 6½" x 6½"
Aqua #2	3 squares, 6½" x 6½"
Dark blue for inner border	6 strips, 1½" x 42"
Red for outer border	7 strips, 6" x 42"
Binding fabric	7 strips, 2½" x 42"

Making the Triangle Squares and Blocks

1. Make the number of each triangle-square color combination shown, following the instructions below for the desired method.

   Method 1: Refer to the instructions on page 6 to make and trim 32 copies of grid 2. If you have cut strips from the fabrics, use the trimmed copies to cut 16 rectangles *each* from the red, dark blue, and yellow solids or small prints; 11 rectangles from the aqua #1 solid or small print; and 5 rectangles from the aqua #2 solid or small print. If you are using individual pieces of fabric, cut them to the same size as the trimmed grids if necessary; use the trimmed grids as a guide.

   Pair a red rectangle with eight yellow rectangles, six aqua #1 rectangles, and two aqua #2 rectangles. Pair each of the remaining yellow and aqua #1 and #2 rectangles with a blue rectangle. Make the triangle squares. Note that you will have six leftover triangle squares each of the red-and-aqua #2, aqua #1-and-blue, blue-and-yellow, and yellow-and-red combinations.

   Method 2: Refer to the instructions on page 7 to pair the red squares with 45 yellow squares, 36 aqua #1 squares, and 9 aqua #2 squares. Pair each of the remaining yellow and aqua #1 and #2 squares with a blue square. Make the triangle squares.

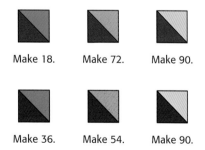

Make 18.   Make 72.   Make 90.

Make 36.   Make 54.   Make 90.

2. Arrange nine identical triangle squares together as shown to make the block. Make the number shown for each color combination.

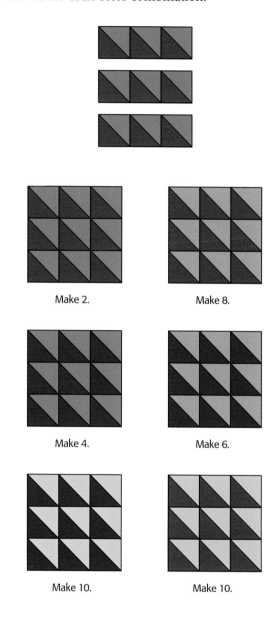

Make 2.   Make 8.

Make 4.   Make 6.

Make 10.   Make 10.

Assembling the Quilt Top

1. Refer to the quilt assembly diagram on page 73 to arrange the blocks and 6½" squares into 10 rows of eight blocks each as shown. Stitch the blocks and squares in each row together, and then stitch the rows together.

2. Refer to "Adding Borders" on page 14 to join and trim the dark blue strips to make inner borders of the correct length. Stitch the top and bottom borders to the quilt top first, and then add the side borders. Repeat with the red outer-border strips.

Finishing

Refer to "Finishing Instructions" on pages 15–18.

1. Layer the quilt top with batting and backing; baste.

2. Quilt as desired.

3. Add a hanging sleeve, if desired.

4. Bind the edges and add a label.

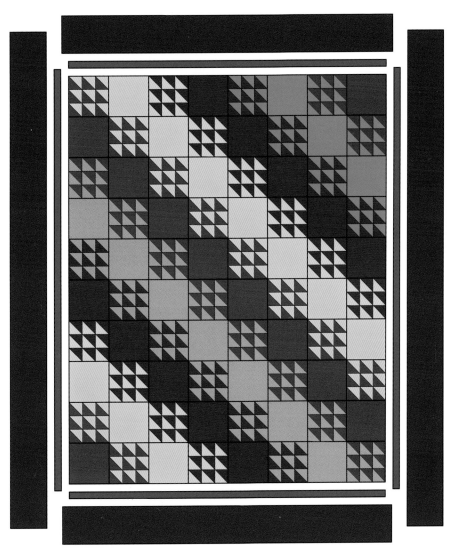

Quilt Assembly Diagram

Transforming Maple Leaves

By Turid Margaret Uren

Can maple leaves be flowers? The inspiration for this quilt came while I was playing with some Maple Leaf blocks. Changing colors and moving them around suddenly made me see flowers and I was on a roll again! Both the flowers and the leaves are made from a lot of scraps (the more the better) to bring this quilt to life.—TURID

FINISHED QUILT SIZE: 52½" x 52½"
FINISHED FLOWER BLOCK SIZE: 12" x 12"
FINISHED LEAF BLOCK SIZE: 6" x 6"

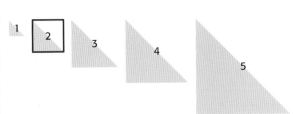

OPTIONS: The blocks can be made in five different size combinations with the grids given at the back of the book. Finished sizes for each block are given below for each grid size.

Grid	Finished Flower Block Size	Finished Leaf Block Size
1	6" x 6"	3" x 3"
2	12" x 12"	6" x 6"
3	18" x 18"	9" x 9"
4	24" x 24"	12" x 12"
5	36" x 36"	18" x 18"

Materials

Yardage is calculated for grid 2 using method 1 and is based on 42"-wide fabric. Refer to "Making Changes" on page 8 to recalculate yardage if you use a grid size other than grid 2.

▲ 1¼ yards *total* of assorted whites for blocks
▲ 1 yard of dark green for outer border
▲ ⅞ yard *total* of assorted greens for blocks
▲ ½ yard *total* of assorted reds for flowers
▲ ⅜ yard of white for inner border
▲ ⅜ yard of medium green for middle border
▲ ¼ yard *each* of assorted blues, purples, and yellows for flowers
▲ ⅝ yard of fabric for binding
▲ 3½ yards of fabric for backing
▲ 57" x 57" piece of batting

Cutting for Triangle Squares

All measurements include ¼"-wide seam allowances.

Fabrics	For method 1, cut:	For method 2, cut:
Assorted reds	16 pieces no smaller than 2⅞" x 2⅞"	16 squares, 2⅞" x 2⅞"
Assorted blues, purples, and yellows	8 pieces no smaller than 2⅞" x 2⅞" of *each* color	8 squares, 2⅞" x 2⅞", of *each* color
Assorted greens*	4 pieces no smaller than 6¼" x 9⅛"; or 48 pieces no smaller than 2⅞" x 2⅞"	48 squares, 2⅞" x 2⅞"
Assorted whites*	4 pieces no smaller than 6¼" x 9⅛" *and* 24 pieces no smaller than 2⅞" x 2⅞"; or 72 pieces no smaller than 2⅞" x 2⅞"	72 squares, 2⅞" x 2⅞"

*Because this quilt is based on using a large amount of scraps, the green-and-white triangle squares are the only triangle squares that can be made using the full grid *without* having a large amount of leftovers. The other color combinations will be made using individual units of the grids. Use the same-sized pieces from the green fabrics that you are using from the white fabrics (6¼" x 9⅛" or 2⅞" x 2⅞").

Cutting for Remaining Pieces

All measurements include ¼"-wide seam allowances.

Fabrics	Size to Cut
Assorted reds	24 squares, 2½" x 2½"
Assorted blues	12 squares, 2½" x 2½"
Assorted purples	12 squares, 2½" x 2½"
Assorted greens	60 squares, 2½" x 2½"
Assorted whites	56 squares, 2½" x 2½"; cut 20 squares in half once diagonally
White for inner border	4 strips, 2½" x 42"
Medium green for middle border	5 strips, 1½" x 42"
Dark green for outer border	5 strips, 5½" x 42"
Binding fabric	6 strips, 2½" x 42"

Making the Triangle Squares and Blocks

1. Make the number of each triangle-square color combination shown, following the instructions below for the desired method.

Method 1: Make 13 copies of grid 2. If you are using the full grid to make the green-and-white triangle squares, refer to the instructions on page 6 to trim eight of the grids; cut the remaining grids apart on the horizontal and vertical lines to make individual units. Discard four individual grid units. If you are using individual squares of all of the fabrics, cut all of the grids apart on the horizontal and vertical lines. Discard four individual grid units. *Individual grid units must be cut exactly on the lines or the triangle squares will not be the correct size.* Trim the fabric pieces to the same size as the grids or grid units you will be using; use the grids and grid units as a guide.

Refer to the instructions on page 6 to pair each green rectangle or square with a white rectangle or square. Pair the remaining white squares with 12 red squares, 6 blue squares, and 6 purple squares. Pair a yellow square with each of the remaining blue, red, and purple squares. Make the triangle squares.

Method 2: Referring to the instructions on page 7 and using the 2⅞" squares, pair a white square with each green square, 12 red squares, 6 blue squares, and 6 purple squares. Pair each yellow square with the remaining blue, red, and purple squares. Make the triangle squares.

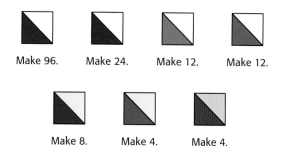

Make 96.   Make 24.   Make 12.   Make 12.

Make 8.   Make 4.   Make 4.

2. To make the Flower blocks, stitch the triangle squares and 2½" squares together as shown to make each flower color. Make the number of each unit as shown.

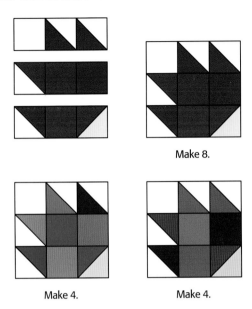

Make 8.

Make 4.   Make 4.

3. Stitch four units from each flower color together as shown. Make two red Flower blocks and one each of the blue and purple.

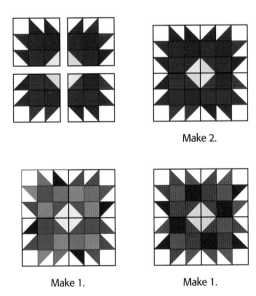

Make 2.

Make 1.   Make 1.

4. To make the Leaf blocks, make 20 copies of the stem foundation pattern on page 79. For each stem square, place the wrong side of a piece of the remaining green fabric against the unprinted

side of the foundation pattern, making sure that it covers section 1 on all sides by at least ¼". Pin the fabric in place from the paper side.

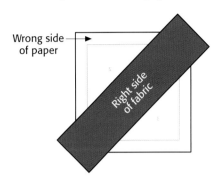

5. With right sides together, place a white triangle over the section 1 piece, making sure that the fabric edge extends past the line between sections 1 and 2 by at least ¼". Position the fabric piece so that when it is stitched down and turned back, section 2 and the seam allowance around it will be completely covered.

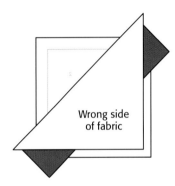

6. Reduce the stitch length on your machine to 18 to 20 stitches per inch. Holding the fabric for section 2 in place, turn the foundation unit to the paper side and stitch along the line between sections 1 and 2, beginning and ending a few stitches beyond both ends of the line.

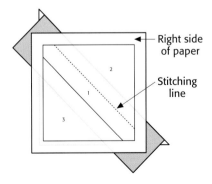

7. With the paper side up, fold back the paper along the seam line and trim the seam allowance to ¼". From the fabric side, press the fabric open so that it covers section 2.

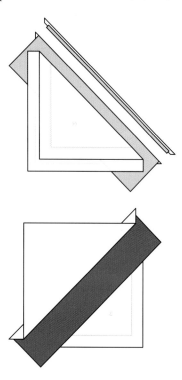

8. Repeat this process for section 3. Turn the completed square to the paper side and trim along the outer line. Do not remove the paper until the quilt top is finished.

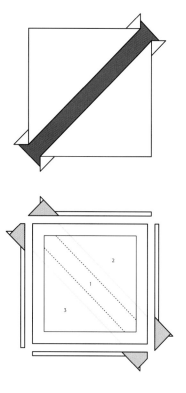

9. Stitch the stem squares, the green-and-white triangle squares, and the remaining green and white 2½" squares together as shown. Make 20.

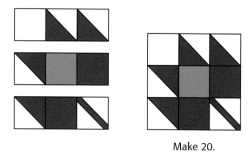

Make 20.

10. Stitch the Leaf blocks into pairs as shown. Make 10.

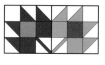

Make 10.

Assembling the Quilt Top

1. Arrange the Flower blocks and leaf pairs into four horizontal rows as shown. Stitch the pieces in each row together, and then stitch the rows together.

2. Refer to "Adding Borders" on page 14 and the quilt assembly diagram to trim the white strips to make inner-border strips of the correct lengths. Stitch the top and bottom borders to the quilt top first, and then add the side borders. Join and trim the medium green strips to make middle borders of the correct lengths. Stitch the top and bottom borders to the quilt top first, and then add the side borders. Repeat with the dark green outer-border strips.

3. Remove the paper from the stem squares.

Finishing

Refer to "Finishing Instructions" on pages 15–18.

1. Layer the quilt top with batting and backing; baste.

2. Quilt as desired.

3. Add a hanging sleeve, if desired.

4. Bind the edges and add a label.

Quilt Assembly Diagram

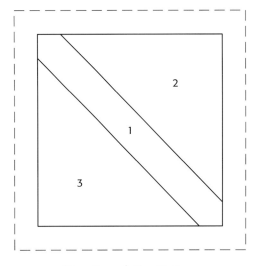

Stem Foundation Pattern

Tea Time

By Kristin Bergljot Johannessen

This quilt is as fresh as the first tulips of spring. I use it as a covering for my garden table. It brings with it a feeling of lazy afternoons, sipping tea from thin china cups. The layout gives the impression of a medallion, when in fact it is a simple, straight-set design.—KRISTIN

FINISHED QUILT SIZE: 56½" x 56½"
FINISHED BLOCK SIZE: 8" x 8"

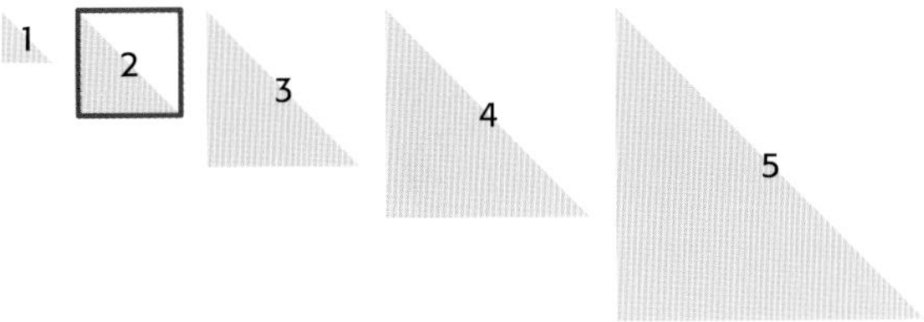

OPTIONS: The blocks can be made in five different sizes with any of the grids given at the back of the book. Finished block sizes are given below for each grid size.

Grid	Finished Block Size
1	4" x 4"
2	8" x 8"
3	12" x 12"
4	16" x 16"
5	24" x 24"

Materials

Yardage is calculated for grid 2 using method 1 and is based on 42"-wide fabric. Refer to "Making Changes" on page 8 to recalculate yardage if you use a grid size other than grid 2.

- ▲ 2½ yards *total* of assorted creams for Tulip blocks and alternate blocks
- ▲ 1 yard *total* of assorted pinks for Tulip blocks
- ▲ ⅞ yard of dark green for outer border
- ▲ ¾ yards *total* of assorted greens for Tulip blocks
- ▲ ¼ yard of dark pink for inner border
- ▲ ⅝ yard of fabric for binding
- ▲ 4 yards of fabric for backing
- ▲ 61" x 61" piece of batting

Cutting for Triangle Squares

All measurements include ¼"-wide seam allowances. You'll be cutting the grids apart in this project so that a variety of scraps can be used without having a large amount of leftover triangle squares.

Fabrics	For method 1, cut:	For method 2, cut:
Assorted pinks	24 pieces no smaller than 2⅞" x 2⅞"	24 squares, 2⅞" x 2⅞"
Assorted greens	24 pieces no smaller than 2⅞" x 2⅞"	24 squares, 2⅞" x 2⅞"
Assorted creams	48 pieces no smaller than 2⅞" x 2⅞"	48 squares, 2⅞" x 2⅞"

Cutting for Remaining Pieces

All measurements include ¼"-wide seam allowances.

Fabrics	Size to Cut
Assorted pinks	96 squares, 2½" x 2½"
Assorted greens	48 squares, 2½" x 2½"
Assorted creams	144 squares, 2½" x 2½" 12 squares, 9¼" x 9¼"
Dark pink for inner border	5 strips, 1" x 42"
Dark green for outer border	6 strips, 4" x 42"
Binding fabric	6 strips, 2½" x 42"

Making the Triangle Squares and Blocks

1. Make 48 triangle squares that are half cream and half pink and 48 triangle squares that are half cream and half green, following the instructions on page 82 for the desired method.

Method 1: Make eight copies of grid 2. Cut each grid apart exactly on the horizontal and vertical lines to make the individual grid units. *Individual grid units must be cut exactly on the lines or the triangle squares will not be the correct size.* Trim the fabric pieces to the same size as the grid units; use the grid units as a guide.

Refer to the instructions on page 6 to pair each pink square and each green square with a cream fabric square. Make the triangle squares.

Method 2: Refer to the instructions on page 7 to pair each pink square and each green square with a cream square. Make the triangle squares.

Make 48. Make 48.

2. To make the Tulip blocks, stitch the triangle squares and 2½" squares together as shown. Make 24. In this project, we made an effort to position a 2½" square that was cut from the same fabric as the green or pink triangle square next to it.

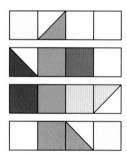 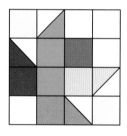

Make 24.

3. To make the alternate blocks, pair each cream 9¼" square with a different cream 9¼" square. Refer to method 2 on page 7 to make the triangle squares. Cut each triangle square in half diagonally as shown. Stitch two different halves together to complete the blocks. Make 12.

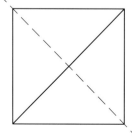 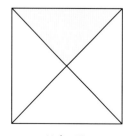

Make 12.

Assembling the Quilt Top

1. Refer to the quilt assembly diagram to arrange the Tulip blocks and alternate blocks into six horizontal rows of six blocks each as shown. Stitch the blocks in each row together, and then stitch the rows together.

2. Refer to "Adding Borders" on page 14 to join and trim the dark pink strips to make inner borders of the correct lengths. Stitch the top and bottom borders to the quilt top first, and then add the side borders. Repeat with the dark green outer-border strips.

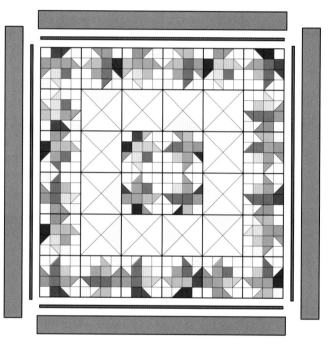

Quilt Assembly Diagram

Finishing

Refer to "Finishing Instructions" on pages 15–18.

1. Layer the quilt top with batting and backing; baste.

2. Quilt as desired.

3. Add a hanging sleeve, if desired.

4. Bind the edges and add a label.

Monkey Wrench?

By Kristin Bergljot Johannessen. Machine quilted by AKD Quilteteknikk.

Take an ordinary Monkey Wrench block, add lots of colors, apply the colors untraditionally, and you've given a whole new look to an old favorite. This was a fun project to make, and I almost went wild with my scraps. I tried a lot of different colors for the border, and I found that the border color I chose enhanced the same color in the blocks. I ended up with a red quilt.—KRISTIN

FINISHED QUILT SIZE: 84½" x 96½"
FINISHED BLOCK SIZE: 12" x 12"

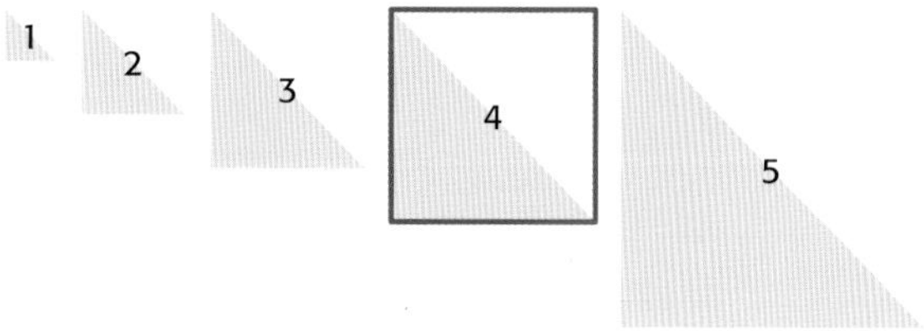

OPTIONS: The blocks can be made in five different sizes with any of the grids given at the back of the book. Finished block sizes are given below for each grid size.

Grid	Finished Block Size
1	3" x 3"
2	6" x 6"
3	9" x 9"
4	12" x 12"
5	18" x 18"

Materials

Yardage is calculated for grid 4 using method 1 and is based on 42"-wide fabric. Refer to "Making Changes" on page 8 to recalculate yardage if you use a grid size other than grid 4.

- ▲ 6 yards *total* of assorted reds, greens, blues, and yellows for blocks
- ▲ 3½ yards *total* of assorted whites and tans for blocks
- ▲ 2 yards of dark red for border
- ▲ 1 yard of fabric for binding
- ▲ 8 yards of fabric for backing (crosswise seams)
- ▲ 89" x 101" piece of batting

Cutting for Triangle Squares

All measurements include ¼"-wide seam allowances.

Fabrics	For method 1, cut:	For method 2, cut:
Assorted reds, greens, blues, and yellows	14 strips, 6" x 42"; or 42 pieces no smaller than 5⅜" x 10¼"	84 squares, 4⅞" x 4⅞"
Assorted whites and tans	14 strips, 6" x 42"; or 42 pieces no smaller than 5⅜" x 10¼"	84 squares, 4⅞" x 4⅞"

Cutting for Remaining Pieces

All measurements include ¼"-wide seam allowances.

Fabrics	Size to Cut
Assorted reds, greens, blues, and yellows	42 strips, 2½" x 42"
Assorted whites and tans	42 squares, 4½" x 4½"
Dark red for border	9 strips, 6½" x 42"
Binding fabric	11 strips, 2½" x 42"

Making the Triangle Squares and Blocks

1. Make 168 triangle squares that are half white or tan and half red, green, blue, or yellow, following the instructions below for the desired method.

   Method 1: Refer to the instructions on page 6 to make and trim 42 copies of grid 4. If you have cut strips from the fabrics, use the trimmed grids to cut 42 rectangles from the assorted red, green, blue, and yellow strips and 42 rectangles from the assorted white and tan strips. If you are using rectangles of fabric, cut them to the same size as the grids; use the trimmed grids as a guide.

   Pair each white or tan rectangle with a red, green, blue, or yellow rectangle. Make the triangle squares.

   Method 2: Refer to the instructions on page 7 to pair each white or tan square with a red, green, blue, or yellow square. Make the triangle squares.

Make 168.

2. Stitch a 2½" x 42" red, green, blue, or yellow strip to a different color 2½" x 42" strip along the long edges as shown to make a strip set. Make 21. Crosscut the strip sets into 168 segments, each 4½" wide.

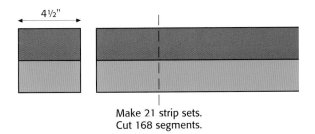

Make 21 strip sets.
Cut 168 segments.

3. Arrange four triangle squares, four units from step 2, and one 4½" square together as shown to make the block. Make 42.

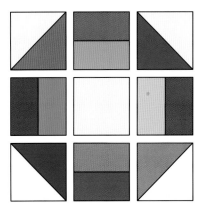

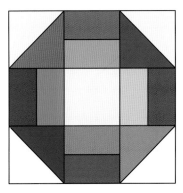

Make 42.

Assembling the Quilt Top

1. Arrange the blocks into seven rows of six blocks each. Stitch the blocks in each row together, and then stitch the rows together.

2. Refer to "Adding Borders" on page 14 to join and trim the dark red strips to make borders of the correct lengths. Stitch the top and bottom borders to the quilt top first, and then add the side borders.

Quilt Assembly Diagram

Finishing

Refer to "Finishing Instructions" on pages 15–18.

1. Layer the quilt top with batting and backing; baste.

2. Quilt as desired.

3. Add a hanging sleeve, if desired.

4. Bind the edges and add a label.

"Traditional Monkey Wrench"
by Kristin Bergljot Johannessen, 30" x 36".

Using just two colors gives this quilt a totally different look from its colorful counterpart. The simplicity allows a pieced border to add interest.

One of My Favorites

By Kristin Bergljot Johannessen

This is one of my favorite designs because it is so versatile and easy to make. I have made it in many different colors and with many different appliqué motifs in the border. The center is pieced from squares the same size as the triangle squares used in the border. I use this particular quilt as a tablecloth. When I'm going to use a quilt as a tablecloth, I use either a very lightweight batting or no batting at all so that it drapes nicely.—KRISTIN

FINISHED QUILT SIZE: 42½" x 42½"
FINISHED BLOCK SIZE: 6" x 6"

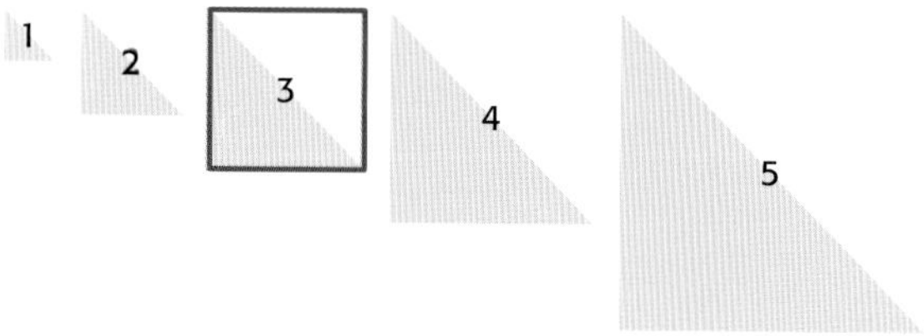

OPTIONS: The blocks can be made in five different sizes with any of the grids given at the back of the book. Finished block sizes are given below for each grid size.

Grid	Finished Block Size
1	2" x 2"
2	4" x 4"
3	6" x 6"
4	8" x 8"
5	12" x 12"

Materials

Yardage is calculated for grid 3 using method 1 and is based on 42"-wide fabric. Refer to "Making Changes" on page 8 to recalculate yardage if you use a grid size other than grid 3.

- ▲ 1⅛ yards *total* of assorted greens for border blocks
- ▲ 1⅛ yards *total* of assorted whites and creams for border blocks
- ▲ ⅝ yard *each* of 5 different red fabrics for quilt-top center squares and heart appliqués
- ▲ ½ yard of fabric for binding
- ▲ 3 yards of fabric for backing
- ▲ 47" x 47" piece of thin batting (optional)
- ▲ ½ yard of paper-backed fusible web

Cutting for Triangle Squares

All measurements include ¼"-wide seam allowances.

Fabrics	For method 1, cut:	For method 2, cut:
Assorted greens	6 strips, 5" x 42"; or 24 pieces no smaller than 4⅜" x 8¼"	48 squares, 3⅞" x 3⅞"
Assorted whites and creams	6 strips, 5" x 42"; or 24 pieces no smaller than 4⅜" x 8¼"	48 squares, 3⅞" x 3⅞"

Cutting for Remaining Pieces

All measurements include ¼"-wide seam allowances.

Fabrics	Size to Cut
5 different reds	20 squares, 3½" x 3½", from *each* red (100 total)
Binding fabric	5 strips, 2½" x 42"

Making the Triangle Squares and Border Blocks

1. Make 96 triangle squares that are half white and half green, following the instructions below for the desired method.

   Method 1: Refer to the instructions on page 6 to make and trim 24 copies of grid 3. If you have cut strips from the fabrics, use the trimmed copies to cut 24 rectangles *each* from the assorted green and assorted white 5" x 42" strips. If you are using individual pieces of fabric, cut them to the same size as the trimmed grids; use the grids as a guide. Pair each green rectangle with a white rectangle. Make the triangle squares.

   Method 2: Refer to the instructions on page 7 to pair each green square with a white square. Make the triangle squares.

Make 96.

2. Stitch four triangle squares together as shown. Make 24.

Make 24.

3. Trace the heart pattern on page 90 onto the paper side of the fusible web 24 times. Cut out the hearts, leaving a generous margin around the outside of each heart. Follow the manufacturer's instructions to fuse each motif to the wrong side of the remainder of the red fabrics. Cut out each heart on the drawn line. Remove the paper backing and center a heart on each unit from step 2 as shown; be sure to rotate the hearts on the four corner blocks. Fuse in place.

Hand or machine stitch around the edges of each heart with a decorative stitch.

Make 20.   Make 4.

Assembling the Quilt Top

1. Arrange the red squares into 10 rows of 10 squares each as shown. Each color should run diagonally across the quilt. Stitch the squares in each row together, and then stitch the rows together.

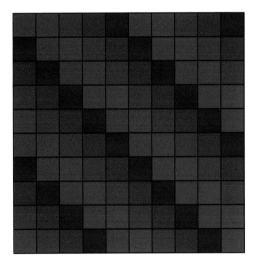

2. Stitch five border blocks together as shown to make the top and bottom borders. Make two. Stitch seven border blocks together as shown to make the side borders. Make two.

Top and Bottom Borders
Make 2.

Side Borders
Make 2.

3. Refer to the quilt assembly diagram to stitch the top and bottom borders to the quilt top first, and then add the side borders.

Quilt Assembly Diagram

Finishing

Refer to "Finishing Instructions" on pages 15–18.

1. Layer the quilt top with batting and backing; baste.

2. Quilt as desired.

3. Add a hanging sleeve, if desired.

4. Bind the edges and add a label.

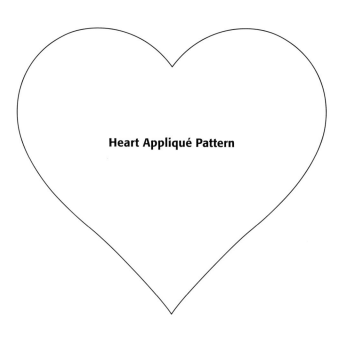

Heart Appliqué Pattern

"Yellow Variation"
by Kristin Bergljot Johannessen, 42½" x 42½".

Change the colors and the motifs to suit your decor or any occasion.

Starry Night

By Turid Margaret Uren

This is my newest work, completed just in time for this book! There is a lot of me in this quilt, and I feel it represents where I stand today. The excitement I feel when a new design comes out of the chaos is worth it all. This may not be the easiest project in the book, but if you use the grids for making the triangle squares, all it takes is some patience!—TURID

FINISHED QUILT SIZE: 44½" x 44½"
FINISHED BLOCK SIZE: 8" x 8"

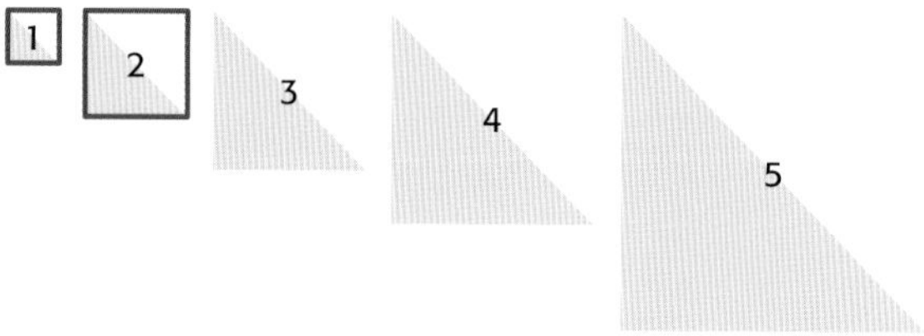

OPTIONS: The blocks can be made in three different sizes with a combination of two of the grids given at the back of the book. Finished block sizes are given below for each grid combination.

Grid Combination	Finished Block Size
1 and 2	8" x 8"
2 and 4	16" x 16"
3 and 5	24" x 24"

Materials

Yardage is calculated for the grid 1-and-2 combination using method 1 and is based on 42"-wide fabric. Refer to "Making Changes" on page 8 to recalculate yardage if you use a combination other than grid 1-and-2.

- ▲ 2½ yards *total* of assorted dark blues for blocks
- ▲ 2 yards *total* of assorted yellows for blocks
- ▲ ¾ yard of dark blue for outer border
- ▲ ⅛ yard *each* of 2 different yellows for inner border
- ▲ ½ yard of fabric for binding
- ▲ 3¼ yards of fabric for backing
- ▲ 49" x 49" piece of batting

Cutting for Triangle Squares

All measurements include ¼"-wide seam allowances.

Note: The triangle squares must be made in groups of eight from the same two fabrics. The rectangle amounts given will produce extra triangle squares but will give you the number of groups required to make the stars. Some preplanning is necessary for the large Star blocks, however. For each of the six stars, you will need eight triangle squares each from grids 1 and 2 that are made using the same yellow fabric. The triangle squares made from grid 1 can be either a yellow-and-yellow combination or a yellow-and-blue combination.

Fabrics	For method 1, cut:	For method 2, cut:
Assorted yellows	12 pieces no smaller than 6⅛" x 9⅞" for use with grid 1	120 squares, 1⅞" x 1⅞"
	6 pieces no smaller than 6¼" x 9⅛" for use with grid 2	24 squares, 2⅞" x 2⅞"
Assorted dark blues	10 pieces no smaller than 6⅛" x 9⅞" for use with grid 1	112 squares, 1⅞" x 1⅞"
	6 pieces no smaller than 6¼" x 9⅛" for use with grid 2	24 squares, 2⅞" x 2⅞"

Cutting for Remaining Pieces

All measurements include ¼"-wide seam allowances.
Note: *Additional pieces will be cut later for the large stars.*

Fabrics	Size to Cut
Assorted yellows and assorted dark blues	24 squares, 2½" x 2½"
Assorted dark blues	96 squares, 1½" x 1½"
	24 squares, 2½" x 2½"
	8 squares, 4½" x 4½"
	4 squares, 4⅞" x 4⅞"; cut each square in half once diagonally to yield 8 half-square triangles
	2 squares, 8⅞" x 8⅞"; cut each square in half once diagonally to yield 4 half-square triangles
	1 square, 9¼" x 9¼"; cut in half twice diagonally to yield 4 quarter-square triangles
Yellows for inner border	2 strips, 1½" x 42", from *each* yellow (4 total)
Dark blue for outer border	5 strips, 4½" x 42"
Binding fabric	5 strips, 2½" x 42"

Making the Triangle Squares and Blocks

1. Make the number of each triangle-square color combination shown, following the instructions below for the desired method.

   Method 1: Refer to the instructions on page 6 to make and trim 11 copies of grid 1 and six copies of grid 2. Cut the fabric pieces to the same size as the grid indicated in the cutting instructions; use the trimmed grids as a guide.

   Pair two different yellow grid 1 rectangles together. Pair each of the remaining grid 1 yellow rectangles with a blue grid 1 rectangle; repeat for the blue and yellow grid 2 rectangles. Make the triangle squares.

   Method 2: Refer to the instructions on page 7 to pair each dark blue square with a yellow square of the same size. Pair the remaining yellow squares together; use two different yellows in each pair. Make the triangle squares.

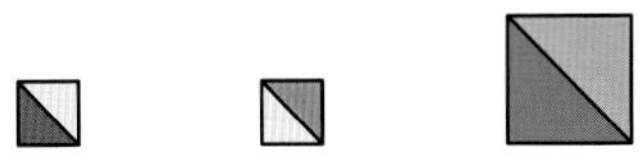

   Make 224.   Make 16.   Make 48.

2. Separate the grid 2 triangle squares into six groups of eight matching triangle squares each. Set aside the remaining grid 2 triangle squares for use in another project. From the grid 1 triangle squares, select eight matching triangle squares for each grid 2 group that were made with the same yellow fabric. For each group, cut four 1½" squares from the same yellow fabric that appears in the grid 1 and grid 2 triangle squares and one 2½" square from the same blue or yellow fabric used in the other half of the grid 1 squares. Set these pieces aside for the large Star blocks.

3. To make the small Star blocks, stitch together eight matching grid 1 triangle squares; four dark blue 1½" squares; and one yellow or dark blue 2½" square as shown. Make a total of 24 units.

Make 24.

4. Stitch three star units and one dark blue 4½" square together as shown. Make six. Stitch two star units and two dark blue 4½" squares together as shown. Make one. Set the remaining star units aside for the half blocks.

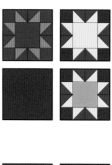 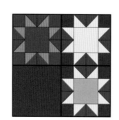

Make 6.

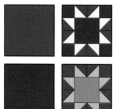 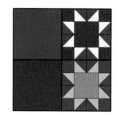

Make 1.

5. To make the large Star blocks, refer to step 3 to make the star unit for the center of each block. Use the pieces you set aside in step 2. Stitch the eight grid 2 triangle squares and four dark blue 2½" squares to the center unit as shown to complete the block. Make a total of six large Star blocks.

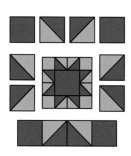 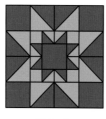

Make 6.

6. To make the half blocks, stitch a dark blue 4⅞" triangle to two adjacent sides of each of the remaining star units from step 4 as shown. Make four.

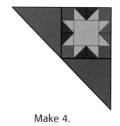

Make 4.

Assembling the Quilt Top

1. Arrange the small Star blocks, the large Star blocks, the half blocks, and the dark blue 8⅞" triangles into five rows as shown. Stitch the pieces in each row together, and then stitch the rows together. Stitch a dark blue 9¼" triangle to each corner.

2. Refer to "Adding Borders" on page 14 to trim the inner-border strips to make inner borders of the correct lengths. Use one yellow for the left side and top border strips and the remaining yellow for the right side and bottom border strips. Stitch the top and bottom borders to the quilt top first, and then add the side borders. Join and trim the dark blue outer-border strips to make borders of the correct lengths. Stitch the top and bottom borders to the quilt top first, and then add the side borders.

Finishing

Refer to "Finishing Instructions" on pages 15–18.

1. Layer the quilt top with batting and backing; baste.

2. Quilt as desired.

3. Add a hanging sleeve, if desired.

4. Bind the edges and add a label.

Quilt Assembly Diagram

ABOUT THE AUTHORS

Kristin Bergljot Johannessen and **Turid Margaret Uren** are sisters with a common passion for patchwork and quilting. For the last three years they have really been "hooked on triangles" and for the purpose of producing triangle squares quickly and easily, they developed the triangle grids used in this book.

Says Kristin:

Growing up in a family where everyone was doing some sort of handcraft, knitting and dressmaking became a natural part of my daily life. When I discovered new and interesting crafts, I had to give each one a try. After I attended my first quilting class in 1983, patchwork became one of my main interests. When Turid and her friends wanted to sell their quilt shop, Quilte Huset, in 1989, I was given the opportunity to buy it. Today I am still in business, now sharing the ownership with a friend. Patchwork and quilting have become part of the way I live and give me new and exciting challenges every day.

Says Turid:

My first encounter with patchwork and quilting happened back in 1979. That was when I moved from Norway with my family to La Porte, a small Texas town. Being a dressmaker, I soon went looking for fabric and by chance happened to walk into a quilt shop. Before long I took my first quilting class, and my life changed forever. Our stay in Texas lasted for five years. I did a lot of patchwork while there and I dreaded the day I had to say good-bye to all of the wonderful quilt shops and quilting fabrics. Back in Bergen, Norway, I opened one of the first quilt shops in Norway in 1984, importing American fabric. Kristin was very much involved in the shop from the start, selling fabric and teaching patchwork classes. The quilting community grew and grew, and in 1987 we founded Norway's first quilt guild, Bergen Quiltelag. My love for patchwork and quilting is as strong today as it ever was, but now I find myself more involved in designing new patterns, and the patterns with triangle squares are among my favorites!

Grid 1
Finished triangle square:
1" x 1"

Grid 2
Finished triangle square: 2" x 2"

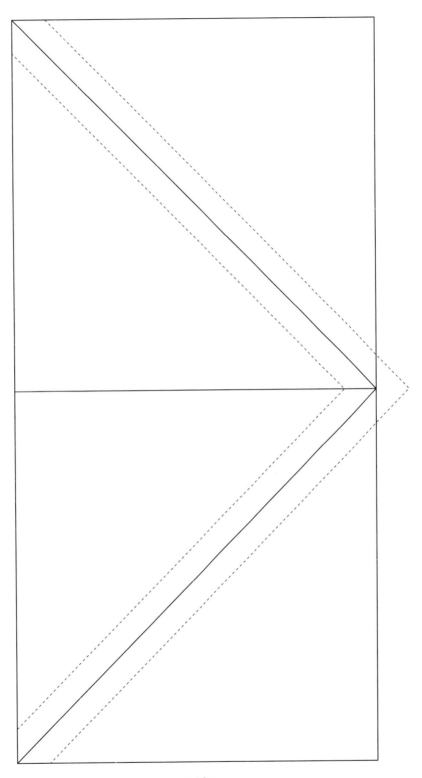

Grid 3
Finished triangle square: 3" x 3"

Grid 4
Finished triangle square: 4" x 4"

Grid 5
Finished triangle square: 6" x 6"